Go MAD
About Negotiating

Achieving results through influencing the
thinking of others

First published in Great Britain in 2006 by
Go MAD Books
Pocket Gate Farm
Off Breakback Road
Woodhouse Eaves
Leicestershire
LE12 8RS

British Library Cataloguing in Publication Data.
A catalogue record for this book is available from the British Library.

ISBN 0-9551287-0-6

Printed and bound in Great Britain by Biddles Ltd, Norfolk.

ACKNOWLEDGEMENTS

Thanks from Jonathan

Thanks to Andy for life-changing inspiration, faith, guidance and coffee.

Thanks to Ken for constant support, editorial brilliance, and fantastic ideas.

Thanks to every negotiator I have ever met, on whatever side of the table – I've learned from you all.

Thanks, and much love, to Helen, for everything, not least patience and humour.

Thanks from Andy

Thanks to Jonathan for developing another application of the Go MAD Framework, persistence and writing most of the book.

Thanks to Ken for patience, coordination and support.

Thanks to Harriett & Gale for the attention to detail.

Thanks to solution focused thinkers everywhere who take action to make a difference.

Cover design by Blueleaf. Thanks to Adrian and the team.

**"What one has, one ought to use;
and whatever he does,
he should do with all his might."
Cicero**

Go MAD® /go mad/v.,n., & adj. abbr. Go Make A Difference. A solution focused thinking system designed to add value to any individual and to any organisation in achieving any difference that they want to make through: greater clarity of thinking; increased speed of thinking; improved creative thinking; to achieve consistency in achieving personal and business goals. Measured business improvement by the structured development and application of people's ability to Make A Difference.

Contents

Page

Thinking during the negotiation

ABOUT THE AUTHORS

Jonathan Donovan is Head of Employee Relations with a leading international mobile phone business and has in-depth experience of achieving results in commercial negotiations in various FTSE 100 businesses. Jonathan has successfully conducted multimillion pound negotiations with business customers and suppliers through to a variety of robust trade union negotiations. Jonathan is passionate about developing people to make a difference through access to pragmatic and highly applicable negotiation tools and techniques.

Andy Gilbert is the developer of the critically acclaimed Go MAD Thinking System. He is passionate about helping people make a difference by developing their ability to think systemically in a solution focused way. Andy is author of over 100 books, videos, and audio programmes including, 'Go MAD – The Art of Making A Difference' and 'Go MAD About Coaching'. As Managing Director of Go MAD Research & Consulting Group, Andy works worldwide designing business improvement programmes for organisations seeking to transform their leadership thinking.

Jonathan first met Andy at a conference in May 2003. Having read a couple of Andy's books and been trained by Andy in solution focused thinking skills, Jonathan realised that the Go MAD Thinking System provided a holistic framework to assist people when negotiating. As an experienced negotiator, Jonathan recognised the importance of thinking skills and asked Andy to design and co-deliver a series of negotiating skills training programmes for managers in his organisation. Following their success, they agreed to undertake further negotiations research together and write their first joint publication, 'How to win in negotiations – 130 ways to make a difference'. This, their second book provides a more step-by-step approach to successful negotiations.

11

"Honest disagreement is often a
good sign of progress."
Mahatma Gandhi

INTRODUCTION

1. Who is this book for?

Hello... And welcome to Go MAD About Negotiating.

This hands-on and highly pragmatic guide starts from the premise that great negotiators are people who have developed the ability to achieve great results by successfully influencing the thinking of others.

This book is aimed at everyone who wants to improve the quality of their influencing and negotiating skills, regardless of their current level of expertise. Using insights from a comprehensive research programme involving people who have made a real difference through negotiation, you will discover what it is that makes negotiators great.

If you want theoretical background, and a heap of multi-dimensional models that can be used to confuse others, this isn't the book for you. If, however, you want a source of inspiration which will flow through into better results for you, starting tomorrow, you've found it. We'll be running through a highly effective way to help you with your thinking as you prepare for your negotiations, move into the negotiations themselves, and go for closure in your deals. We'll give you handy tools, hints and tips which are drawn from our own experience, and the experience of others. And we'll share the answers to the most commonly asked questions about conducting successful negotiations.

Enjoy making a difference!

2. Getting the most from this book

Let's spend a few moments understanding how this book is structured and then we will share a few ideas, which you might consider useful, about how to get the most from it.

There are five main parts to this book:

Part one provides an overview understanding of the Go MAD Thinking System including the background research, seven Go MAD Key Principles, Go MAD Framework and how it can be applied to negotiating.

Part two focuses on thinking ahead before the negotiation. We explain how to apply each element of the Go MAD Thinking System to fully prepare for a successful negotiation. This includes ways of anticipating how others will think and planning how you could possibly influence their thinking.

Part three concentrates on the actual negotiation with particular emphasis on the importance of asking high quality questions to help yourself and influence others to move forward with their thinking. The Go MAD Thinking System is also used as a diagnostic framework to identify and resolve potential problems during the negotiation.

Part four highlights a few key points to think about following a negotiation to ensure actions are followed through and future negotiations are successful.

Part five contains the answers to over 80 commonly asked questions relating to negotiations, together with several case-studies and further information about applying Go MAD as a solution focused thinking system.

This book blends research with practicality and, in simple steps, we will guide you through the three key stages of negotiation:

- Thinking before the negotiation
- Thinking during the negotiation
- Thinking following the negotiation

We emphasise the importance of thinking as our thoughts form the basis of our actions and ultimately the results we achieve. Once you are familiar with the Go MAD Thinking System, which will be explained shortly, you will easily be able to understand how negotiations based upon a cognitive solution focused approach are likely to have such a high probability of success.

The chapters are deliberately short so that you can always finish reading to the end of a chapter in a few minutes.

We have also included many of our favourite quotes throughout the book. Each is relevant to the theme of that particular part of the book and is provided for inspiration or reflection. For example:

"Don't find a fault, find a remedy."
Henry Ford

If this is your personal copy of the book, you are encouraged to write in it. The margins are deliberately wide to provide space for making notes and the questions and reminders included are there to stimulate your thinking.

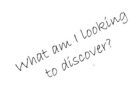
What am I looking to discover?

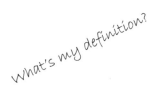

3. What do we mean by 'negotiating'?

Our simple definition of negotiating is, **'Achieving results by influencing the thinking of others'**. That is, engaging in some form of communication with some other person with the aim of winning them round to your point of view.

This, in fact, describes any influencing situation. Does this mean that negotiating, and influencing, are the same thing, and require application of the same skill set? Let's explore this further.

This book is based on comprehensive research involving many hours of interviews with people who have made a real difference in their lives as negotiators in many diverse fields – people who negotiate multimillion pound commercial deals, through to people who negotiate for the release of hostages, or even peace negotiations in the Middle East. One of the areas that struck us as significant was this core question about the relationship between influencing and negotiating, which takes us to the very heart of what exactly negotiating is.

But what makes this important? As with almost all of the issues and questions surrounding what many see as a twilight world of negotiation, this is simple to articulate. We found that many people believe that negotiation is a process that takes place behind closed doors, by highly skilled practitioners who are almost practising a dark art. A world into which the uninitiated cannot go, or indeed fear to tread. We talked to many negotiators and, whilst they recognise the image that some people portray them as having, they don't recognise it from the inside.

The answer to this apparent quandary lies, at least in part, in the fact that many negotiations do indeed often take place behind closed doors. Negotiations, of whatever kind, are often highly sensitive, for commercial or other reasons. There is a saying that if more than two people know something, it's not a secret any more. In their desire to maintain confidentiality, at least for the time being, those who are not involved in a negotiation are not on the list of people who need to know what is going on in the negotiation. So, this looks mysterious. Hence, some people feel that they will never make good negotiators, for many different reasons – it's out of their league, or they'll never be allowed into the inner circle, or they just plain don't want to because they don't believe they have the required skills to become a successful negotiator.

Let's uncover the secrets!

"What you see and hear depends a good deal on where you are standing; it also depends on what sort of person you are."
C.S. Lewis

Our contention is that the mystery might be a very necessary part of the negotiating game, but it isn't actually true in reality.

4. Everyone can negotiate

Let's imagine a person who claims that they can't negotiate. If we ask the question, "Can you remember an occasion where you successfully changed someone's point of view on something?" they will say they can, without exception. So, everyone can negotiate, they just don't know it yet… or they just forgot how to.

Children are great at getting their own way. Take the case of a child who wants to influence the thinking of a parent, say around the purchase of some favoured toy for a birthday. They will hint, ask, beg, cajole, persist, tell stories about their friends who have got one, and even offer

17

When am I most successful in influencing others?

rewards – "I'll clean your car every week if you buy me a..." Children have an unparalleled ability to identify the tactic that will work best in any given situation. And if they don't get their way, they'll attempt to make life miserable for their parent, at least for a while. And then – guess what? – they'll go onto the next thing and they'll still bring it up: "If you get me a... then I won't ever mention the other thing again." Does this sound familiar? It should. You were a child once, and chances are this is somewhere close to what you used to do.

Have you ever heard the phrase 'negotiating the traffic'? It's not called that by accident! If you think about it, driving a car is a complex, non-verbal (usually!) interaction between people who broadly follow a set of rules – speed limits, red lights, the right way round a roundabout and so on. Good drivers spend much of their mental energy on second guessing what move other people are going to make next, and in reacting to that. And motivation is high – you want to get where you are going, safely, and without denting your car or frightening your passengers. All of these elements are found, to some degree, in any influencing or negotiating situation. So if you can drive, or even if you can imagine driving, then you have the skills it takes to make a great negotiator. Maybe you just don't know it yet.

5. I'm an experienced negotiator – what's in it for me?

Imagine your negotiations experience as a patchwork quilt assembled from the component parts you have gathered throughout your life. This includes the knowledge, skills, behaviours, attitudes and other qualities you have developed and learned from others. Think back to the things you have experienced as you have succeeded in your negotiations. All great negotiators have picked up pieces of their own personal patchwork quilt from others – people who they have negotiated with; people in their own team; people they have heard about – and the way they have said or done different things to achieve results. This is the concept of the patchwork quilt – we are the sum total of our experiences and, just as with a real patchwork quilt, some of the early pieces may be covered by later pieces.

**"The more I learn,
the more I realise I don't know."
Albert Einstein**

If you read with a purpose – to discover something you can practically apply – we believe you will find something of value in this book to add to your existing patchwork quilt.

6. The importance of standing for something

What do we mean by this?

Our research shows that all great negotiators have a sense of the personal values they aim to live by – typically, a sense of self-worth and a belief that they add value to their organisations and achieve their personal goals through what they do; they are typically honest, and often far more open – even with people on the other side of the negotiating table – than you might at first imagine to be the case. They generally rate themselves as good communicators, with a strong sense of self-awareness about how they are perceived by others, coupled with a refined ability to read body language and intonation, not just the meaning on the face of – and underneath – words that are said or written. They are generally adept at recognising the value of building relationships with people, even if those relationships are of a short-term nature. They

How do I compare with great negotiators?

19

will go out of their way to be helpful to people with whom they have developed long-term and mutually advantageous relationships. It is not unusual for an experienced negotiator to spend more time helping the other side to sell a deal to their people than he or she spends selling an outcome to their own side; they recognise when this is helpful, and when that degree of investment is needed to cement a deal.

What values underpin my negotiations?

None of this can be achieved, other than in the very short-term, by people who do not stand for something, and who do not therefore live by a code of clear personal values. Negotiation is as much about trust, honesty and integrity as it is about understanding facts and figures. That old adage that a salesperson first needs to sell themselves to their potential client is absolutely true. Negotiators who do not have integrity have nothing – maybe they'll get a deal or two, but their reputation will soon precede them, and they will become all too familiar with the sound of closing doors, and receding possibilities.

These days, even the second-hand car salespeople want you to come back; repeat business, and personal recommendations is their lifeblood and, in this most competitive of environments, often the difference between business success, and business failure.

There is another saying which is particularly powerful, and an absolute must: never, ever, delegate responsibility for your personal integrity as a negotiator to someone else. Nobody will look after your integrity, and your reputation, as well as you do. So do it yourself, and always hold to what you believe in. You know what that is, if you look yourself in the eye and are honest with yourself. Nobody who is anything other than honest with themselves can ever be a great negotiator – they can't hide it for ever.

**"Integrity is doing the right thing,
even if nobody is watching."
Jim Stovall**

Every great negotiator stands for something. There are no exceptions to this. It's as reliable as the laws of physics. Of course, not every negotiator is great, but we're concerned with how to be a great negotiator, not an ordinary one.

7. The three stages of negotiation

There are three distinct stages in any negotiation, no matter what it is about:

* Before the negotiation starts;
* During the negotiation; and
* After the negotiation is over.

In order to strengthen the likelihood of a successful outcome, we will take a systematic approach covering the following key areas:

* Thinking Ahead About the Negotiation;
* Thinking During the Negotiation;
* Thinking Following the Negotiation.

Thinking leads to actions which lead to results.

Great negotiators recognise that each area is every bit as important as the other. It is a matter of constant curiosity as to why some people, embarking on an important journey to influence the thinking of others, don't bother with the first of the three stages. For some, this is about arrogance; for others, ignorance. The fact is that nobody who is arrogant or ignorant is going to become a great negotiator until they truly learn to appreciate the importance of the preparation which needs to be done before a negotiation starts.

A common trap: negotiating is more than the actual negotiation.

Taking this approach will avoid two specific, and potentially very costly, traps – neither of which may be immediately obvious to the less experienced negotiator.

The first trap is to wrongly assume that negotiation is about the direct interaction between the parties who are seeking to reach a deal. This is reinforced, almost subconsciously, by the language we frequently use. We meet someone coming out of a discussion and we ask them, "How did the negotiations go?" It is as if the discussions themselves are the only part of the negotiation.

In fact, the discussions are the second of three phases. The first phase – thinking before the negotiation – and the third phase – thinking after the negotiation – are all part of the negotiations. Each has an important role to play in achieving success.

"Change favours the prepared mind."
Louis Pasteur

This leads us neatly to the second trap. This is the trap of believing that we have reached the optimum deal, the best available outcome, through a negotiation, when in fact we have not. This is a difficult one; how do you know, at the end of a negotiation, whether you have reached the most advantageous outcome you could possibly have reached, taking into account all the ways in which you would wish to measure success? These could include:

*   The actual terms of the deal: price, time-scales for delivery, quality standards, payment terms and dates, implementation time-scales, any communication arrangements and so on, as appropriate;
*   The degree to which those people who are important to you for whatever reason are satisfied with your achievements;

- Any implications for your personal reward, and that of your team, through commissions, bonuses, percentage of value added and the like;
- The degree to which the deal has strengthened the relationship between you and the other party, where development of a long-term and mutually advantageous relationship is important;
- The degree to which your standing and reputation as an effective negotiator has been maintained or improved.

What are my possible measures of success?

The answer to this quandary lies in getting solid foundations in place before the negotiations start, in identifying all the steps that you can take to position yourself for success both before the talks start, and as the negotiations progress, and in finalising all of the important details once the talks themselves are concluded.

Once the importance of each of the three stages of negotiation is recognised, the rest falls into place, and can more easily be achieved through the systematic application of the tools and techniques set out in this book.

"**Whatever you think, be sure it is what you think;
Whatever you want, be sure it is what you want;
Whatever you feel, be sure that it is what you feel.**"
T. S. Eliot

PART ONE: THE GO MAD THINKING SYSTEM

8. Go MAD – The background research

If you haven't worked it out yet, the initials M.A.D. are an abbreviation of the words Make A Difference. Whenever this phrase is used in this book it includes all differences, large and small, personal and work related.

You have made thousands of differences in your life and continue to make differences each and every day. However, most people are unaware of what they naturally do whenever they achieve success in life. So in January 1998 Andy led what researchers call, a phenomenological research project (i.e. studying the phenomenon of making a difference). The original research question was, **"What is the simplest way of explaining the success process that people naturally use when making a difference?"** (What he discovered was not a process, but a thinking system. However, more about that later.) Ian Chakravorty, a full-time researcher, armed with a tape recorder and notepad, set off around the U.K. to interview people who had made a difference. Andy initially introduced Ian to three people, who he considered had made a difference, for him to interview. They each introduced Ian to three further people, whom they considered had made a difference, whom in turn provided similar introductions. Other people were interviewed as a result of reading or hearing about the differences they had made.

There were no criteria for specifying what the difference should be. Hence, these differences encompassed a wide range of successful activities: commercial, career, balanced lifestyle, political, family, community, educational, personal relationships and many more. Some differences were on a large-scale, others much smaller. All were significant to the individuals making the difference.

Meanwhile, Andy headed up a team of eight consultants researching the differences made by individuals in the workplace. A variety of organisations from the public, private and voluntary sectors were invited to nominate individuals who had made a difference. The range of occupations was diverse and included people of all ages and levels within the organisations. The differences they had made included: doubling the sales turnover of a company; providing exceptional customer care; increasing production by 100%; managing organisational change; enhancing their career; developing others; and implementing a variety of cost saving initiatives. For two months each research interview was filmed as Andy sought to understand the key success principles which were commonly being applied in order to achieve results.

By the end of the year an incredible amount of information had been gathered from a diverse range of sources, all of which related to how individuals successfully made a difference. The research team continually re-listened to each recorded interview, analysed the film footage and studied relevant background reading material. From all of this, emerged a book, 'Go MAD – The Art of Making A Difference', and a practical, easy to understand framework for success comprising seven key principles, which are outlined in the following chapter.

It is at this point that Go MAD moves from being a simple list of seven key principles to a more sophisticated framework, with eleven critical links between the key principles. Furthermore, this framework encompasses a variety of skills and personal competencies that each person can choose to develop further in order to improve their ability to make a difference.

As the use of the Go MAD Framework has grown over the years, Andy had several major realisations. Firstly, that Go MAD is not a process but a system comprised of interdependent components, and understanding the relationship between them is as important as applying each of the key principles. Secondly, that whilst the Framework can be understood and applied very easily by almost everyone at a personal level, there are more in-depth applications for large-scale change and business improvement programmes. "Structured common sense" and, "Simple, yet sophisticated" are two phrases that many people use to describe Go MAD. The third, and most important, realisation provided a major breakthrough in the way that the Go MAD Framework is applied – using it as a 'Thinking System', for individuals to help themselves and others develop their thinking in a solution focused way.

So the answer to the question, "What is Go MAD?" can be summarised as follows: Go MAD is a series of key principles; a framework; a thinking system and a robust set of skills – all of which can be learned and applied by any person to make a difference. In essence, Go MAD has evolved into a development tool applicable to any situation, including an obvious application – negotiations. Now if this sounds a little complicated – relax! All will become clear as we explain this in an easy to understand way over the next few chapters.

9. The Go MAD Key Principles

The following seven key principles are the basic components of your natural framework for being successful:

1. **Having a strong reason why** – it takes a strong reason why to maintain motivation and commitment.

Seven key principles for success.

2. **Defining your goal** – be clear on what you want to achieve, so you can measure your success.
3. **Planning your priorities** – having completed the why and the what this principle moves you onto the how. Generate ideas, consider possibilities, prioritise and plan in the time to achieve your goal.
4. **Having self-belief** – have you got what it takes? The knowledge, skills, resources and confidence. Develop the self-belief that you can make a difference.
5. **Involving others** – you will achieve the greatest results by working with others and obtaining their buy-in.
6. **Taking personal responsibility** – be accountable, a role model to others and make your own choices.
7. **Taking action and measuring the results.**

Principle One considers WHY you want to make a difference.

Principle Two focuses on WHAT difference you want to make.

Principles Three – Seven concentrate on HOW to make the difference.

Many people have commented, "Andy, this is common sense." And, of course, it is! It is also day-to-day common practice for the hundreds of small differences we make. Let's consider an example of how you have applied these principles to make a difference in the past 24 hours.

1. "I'm getting hungry." = Strong reason to make a difference.
2. "I'm going to get something to eat within the next 30 minutes." = Defined goal.
3. "Should I buy some food or prepare a meal?" = Planning priorities.
4. "I've got sufficient time and money." = Self-belief.
5. "Who will prepare or buy my food?" = Involve others.

6. "It's down to me to decide and make time to eat."
    = Personal responsibility.
7. "Meal over and I am no longer hungry." = Action taken
    and results measured.

If everyone uses these key principles naturally, what is the point of Go MAD and this book? Well, hopefully the answer is obvious. If not, here are several thoughts to consider:

People do not apply this thinking consistently – especially at work and when negotiating.
People are largely unaware of this natural thinking for the small differences they repetitiously make.
People can be helped to become consciously aware of what is helping/hindering their success.
People can improve their probability of success when negotiating through the application of proven success principles.

10. The Go MAD Framework

The following diagram provides a useful framework to consciously apply the key principles and start to understand the links between them.

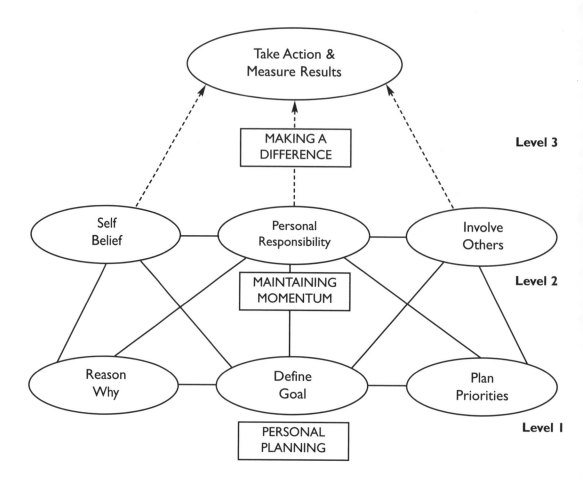

The Go MAD Framework

Notice the three levels of the pyramid. The first level is referred to as **personal planning** and it links principles one, two and three. These are the foundations upon which success is built. It takes a **strong reason why** (principle one) to maintain motivation, face challenges and overcome obstacles. Hence, this is a cornerstone. The other cornerstone is provided by a well-constructed **plan of priorities** (principle three). These principles are linked by having a **defined goal** (principle two) to centrally support the remaining four principles.

Priorities cannot be planned without a defined goal, and the goal cannot be achieved without a strong enough reason to make a difference. With these foundations in place, a second level can be built.

The second level is referred to as **maintaining momentum** and this builds upon the personal planning of the foundation level. Having the **self-belief** (principle four) to succeed in making a difference is dependent upon having a defined goal which, you believe, is possible to achieve. Without the self-belief and the desire to achieve, progress will falter. Hence, the link between principles one and four.

Involving others (principle five) should be built into the plan and prioritised. However, to do it successfully takes both skill and effort in order to continue moving in the right direction. The defined goal and plan of priorities established at the foundation level will need to be communicated and both might need to be revised following the involvement of others. Without this involvement, and the additional support it brings, it might be impossible to move to the next level.

At the centre of the framework is the choice every individual has of taking **personal responsibility** for their actions (principle six) to make a difference. If this choice is exercised then the other key principles, with which it links, stand a chance of being applied. However, in order to move to the third level all of the first six principles have to be in place.

The third level is that of **making a difference** and can only be reached by building the foundations with the first three principles and maintaining the momentum by applying principles four, five and six. Even then, it is still necessary to **take action and measure the results** (principle seven) to know that the goal has been achieved and a difference has been made.

11. SITBACC – 11 critical links

To effectively use the Go MAD Framework as a negotiator, it is important to understand in more detail the eleven critical links between the first six key principles. The mnemonic SITBACC is a useful reminder of these. Starting at the reason why, follow the arrows between the first five key principles to spell SITBAC. The final C of this mnemonic represents the five choice lines that link personal responsibility to the other key principles.

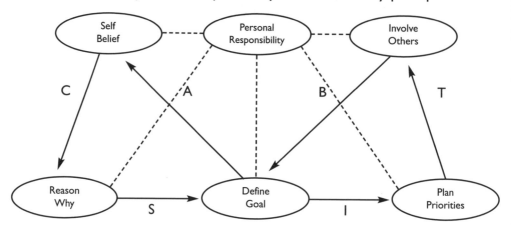

Strength
Importance
Task
Buy-in
Achievability
Check
Choices x5 (indicated by dotted lines)

The link between the first and second key principle is known as the *Strength* line.

To make a difference, the reason for making that difference has to be sufficiently strong. It is not good enough to have a reason and simply know what it is; it has to be powerful enough to survive any potential setbacks. A goal without a strong reason why will not be pursued in times of difficulty.

"Necessity is the mother of skill."
Plato

The link between the second and third key principle is referred to as the *Importance* line.

Planning priorities is a three-stage process of generating possibilities, prioritising those possibilities and planning in time to do the important ones. In order to prioritise it is necessary to refer back to the defined goal to determine which possibility is most important. Hence the link.

The link between the third and fifth key principle is referred to as the *task* line.

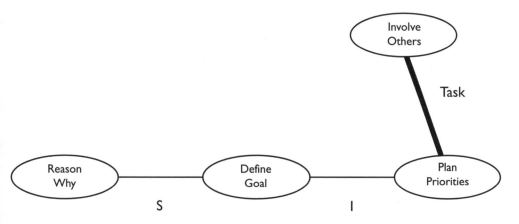

The first stage of the planning priorities process involves generating and exploring possibilities about several things. These include possible tasks to undertake, possible people to involve and possible ways in which they could help, as well as identifying possible obstacles and ways of overcoming them.

"The future belongs to people who see possibilities before they become obvious."
Theodore Leavitt

The link between the second and fifth key principle is referred to as the *Buy-in* line.

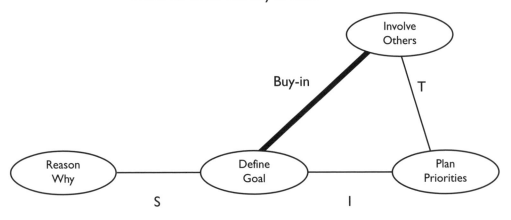

To get others involved in helping to achieve your goal you will first need to get them to buy-in to it being worthwhile. Notice, in the Go MAD Framework, that there is no direct link between your reason why (principle one) and involving others (principle five). The conduit is via the defined goal. In other words, you need to be able to communicate to others not just what you want to achieve, but also why that difference is important to you. Hence the Buy-in line refers to the use of communication and influencing skills. In order to obtain this buy-in from others it might be necessary, on occasions, to redefine your goal in order to make it more acceptable to them and obtain essential support. This is part of the art of negotiating.

> **"The major problem in communication is the illusion that it has occurred."**
> **Albert Einstein**

The link between the second and fourth key principle is known as the *Achievability* line.

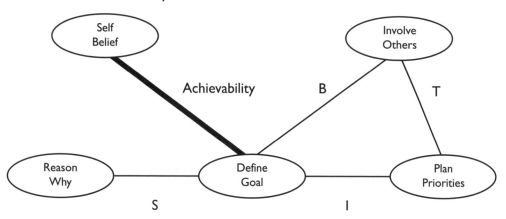

This is an assessment of how achievable you believe your goal to be, i.e. to what extent do you believe you have got what it takes in order to achieve the difference? To answer this question it is necessary to consider the timescale of the goal and level of achievement that has been defined, together with your level of skill, knowledge, available resources and confidence.

> **"If I have the belief that I can do it, I shall surely acquire the capacity to do it even if I may not have it at the beginning."**
> **Mahatma Gandhi**

The link between the first and fourth key principle is referred to as the *Check* line.

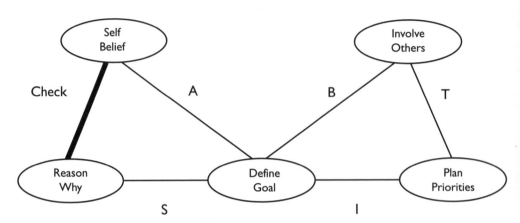

It is common during a negotiation for both parties' levels of self-belief to change or fluctuate. Likewise, the strength of reason why can alter. In order to make a difference an individual needs to maintain high levels of both self-belief and reason why. One without the other will not suffice. Hence, the need to check these levels at various stages when negotiating.

**"He who fears he will suffer,
already suffers from his fear."
Michael de Montaigne**

The sixth key principle is linked to the first five key principles by separate *Choice* lines.

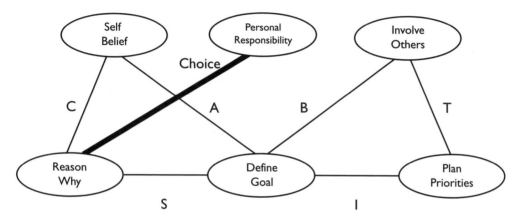

You have to take personal responsibility for choosing whether or not to think about your level of motivation and reasons for wanting to make a difference. Can you be bothered? If so, how strongly?

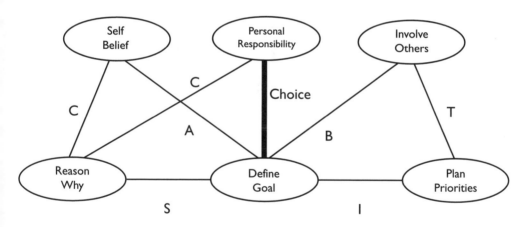

You have to choose how well-defined your goal is. Will you take personal responsibility for turning a vague aim or wish into a specific, measurable, time-dated goal? It's your choice.

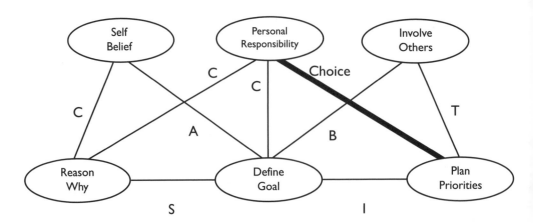

You also have to take personal responsibility for generating possibilities and deciding exactly how much time you will spend on each priority. How much time have you chosen to set aside in your diary to plan for your negotiation?

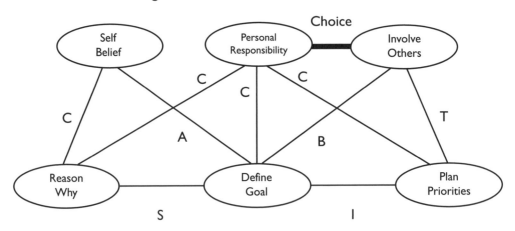

You decide who to involve; what to involve others in; how, when and where to involve others; and how to obtain their buy-in. There are many choices to be made if you are prepared to take personal responsibility for making a difference.

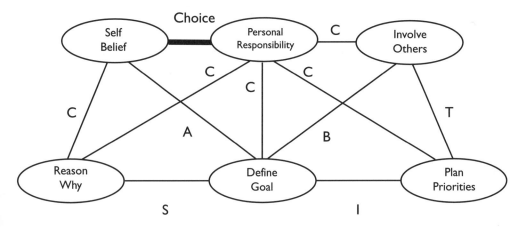

We often refer to this link as the choice we have to make about taking responsibility for our own development. This final choice line links principles four and six together. Are you prepared to assess your capabilities, confidence, knowledge, skills and experience and to ask yourself the question, "Have I got what it takes?"

If the answer is "No", are you prepared to take personal responsibility for developing yourself?

So there you have it – the first six key principles and the eleven critical links between them – seventeen elements of the Go MAD Framework. Before you read any further, it is important to consolidate your understanding and assess your learning so far.

What have I discovered or realised about making a difference?

12. Applying the Go MAD Thinking System to negotiations

The previous section explained the Go MAD Thinking System. Whether you are new to Go MAD Thinking, or have studied the Go MAD Thinking System, either through books or by attending an accredited training programme, you will now appreciate the power available to you by applying what you instinctively do to situations that are not so familiar.

The following section applies the Go MAD Thinking approach to developing your negotiation skills, regardless of your level of expertise. By applying these tools and techniques to your thinking, you will improve your capacity to get great results, every time — results that are measurable, and which you, and others, will wish to celebrate.

TIME TO REFLECT

Before you delve into the detail of the following section, just pause to reflect on your learning from this section. Consider the following questions.

What difference do I want to make?

What have I realised about my own ability to make a difference?

How could I use this when negotiating?

What else have I discovered?

PART TWO: THINKING AHEAD BEFORE THE NEGOTIATION

13. Preparation is everything

Applying the Go MAD Thinking System to your preparations before a negotiation even starts is going to make all the difference between a great achievement or, at best, an adequate outcome and, at worst, failure. This is not rocket science. It's about applying thinking, planning and analytical skills which we all have inherently, in a systemic way to improve the options available to you, to help you understand your motives and the motives of others, and to define your goals in a way that is supported by all the key people whose support you need.

There is no alternative to preparation: it truly is the key to maximising your success. For some, negotiation is all about the cut and thrust of the debate and discussion – there is always a role for the adrenaline junky who lives on the edge. However, great negotiators may sometimes look as if they are flying by the seat of their pants, making it up as they go along – and if you do this, you may just get lucky, once or twice – but they're not.

Great negotiators have done their homework before they get in the room. They know their own team and have defined the roles for each of them, they know who they are facing across the table as best they can in the circumstances, and they have all the facts and figures they need at their disposal. They will have rehearsed their arguments, and will have anticipated as many things that might possibly happen through the course of the negotiation as they can imagine. They will have prepared their opening position, their preferred point of settlement, and their bottom line. They will have worked to understand the range within which a deal may be reached, and will understand their negotiating mandate. Great

What could I possibly improve?

41

negotiators know that you get a better crop from a field if you have prepared the ground properly, and they'll have done their groundwork properly and fully.

Task focused people want to get on and do. Preparation isn't always seen as particularly sexy. We'll change this perception by demonstrating that preparation, prior to a negotiation, is fruitful, productive, and directly leads to better results. One of the key advantages of the Go MAD Thinking approach is that it provides discipline and structure to preparation, and guides how to do it properly.

For now, remember this: the negotiator who has prepared the best has the best chance of success.

14. Knowing your reason why

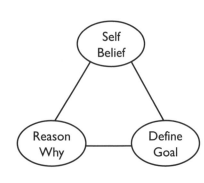

Experienced practitioners of the Go MAD Thinking System will appreciate that there is no specific order in which you should apply each key principle. In fact, the internal triangle of Reason Why, Define Goal, and Self-Belief are closely linked, and each has a strong impact on the other: for example, a goal which is very clearly defined can help to strengthen your self-belief, especially when linked to a very strong Reason Why.

For the purposes of negotiation, however, assessing the strength of your Reason Why can prove an extremely good place to start the process of planning for your negotiation – or even for planning how you are going to influence others who may be requiring you to carry out the negotiation.

Great negotiators know the importance to themselves of what they are there to do – they understand their Reason Why, and appreciate that without a strong Reason Why, the likelihood of success is seriously diminished. In other words, in order to maximise your opportunities for success, you have to have a strong Reason Why determining your involvement in any negotiating or influencing situation.

"Always bear in mind that your own resolution to succeed is more important than any one thing."
Abraham Lincoln

This doesn't mean that consideration of your Reason Why is the first thing you do – it may well not be. Typically, thinking about your goal – that is, the desired outcome from the negotiation – is the first thing you think about. But focusing at an early stage on your Reason Why is an extremely important part of your preparation.

Understanding your Reason Why for going into an influencing or negotiating position is really quite critical. We know that there are different things that motivate us – some motivations originate externally, some come from within. Some external motivations are readily embraced by us, some are forced upon us. Let's illustrate this.

Imagine you are standing in a room, next to a wall. Only it isn't a wall, it's the side of an enormous block of ice, and you can feel the coldness of the air around the block of ice, and within moments you are distinctly uncomfortable. Across the other side of the room is a blazing log fire with a dog asleep, curled up on a rich warm rug in front of it. You can imagine that the dog's thick fur coat is hot to the touch – but the dog is quite comfortable, it seems to like it that way.

You are freezing by now, and you want to be where the dog is, because it's lovely and warm over there. So you take a couple of paces towards the fire, and the first thing you notice is that you're already warming up – even just a few paces away from the big block of ice it isn't that cold any more. You take another pace or two. Actually, you think to yourself, this is pretty good here. I'm about the right temperature now. I'll stay here. In fact, you think to yourself, it's probably too hot over there by the fire, and in any event, I don't know what that dog is like – it might not be friendly. Here will do just fine…

What's wrong with that story? (Other than maybe the bit about the block of ice in the room – we know that doesn't happen!) Firstly, your initial Reason Why, or motivation, was to get away from the cold. This was then interpreted in terms of going over to the fire. But as soon as you had solved your first Reason Why, that is, you'd stopped being cold, you had satisfied your original demand. More often than not, when people do this exercise on our negotiation and influencing strategy workshops, they readily admit that they thought their Reason Why was to go over to the fire, when in fact it wasn't. The point is straightforward when illustrated in this way – learn to understand your REAL reason why, not the one that might look the most obvious.

But why, in the world of negotiations, is this important?

You have to have the right personal motivation for going into a negotiation, because if you do not, it can impact the whole of your internal triangle – this is the combination of your Reason Why, your Defined Goal, and your Self-Belief. Think of the ice example – we have already seen the potential for confusion in the Reason Why. The Goal is equally confused – is the goal to go over to the fireplace, or is it simply to get warm? For a moment it clearly looked as if the goal was to get to the fire. However, once the need to step away from the ice, and therefore warm up, had been satisfied, the need to get over to the fire diminished. Then in came the thought about what the dog might be like, and suddenly the fire wasn't looking so

Am I moving towards or away from something?

attractive. And, as the goal had never been truly articulated in terms of getting to the fire, the chances of achieving the goal were diminished to the point of non-achievement. Finally, you might have had a strong sense of belief that you could get to the fire, but you were even more certain of your ability to get warm. Having achieved that, the sense of self-belief began to ooze away at the thought of a potentially vicious dog. Let sleeping dogs lie, take the easy route...

**"We must ask where we are and
wither we are tending."
Abraham Lincoln**

Imagine you are walking into a negotiation. You aren't sure what your Reason Why is. There is some confusion regarding the Defined Goal. Your Self-Belief, and that of your team, is questionable. This is not a recipe for success. The only people celebrating after the negotiation will be... them. You'll be too busy thinking about how you are going to report back...

This is why your Reason Why is so important. Ask yourself these questions:

- What are my reasons for being in this negotiating situation?
- What is my strongest reason? How strong is that reason for entering into these negotiations?

Accomplished negotiators are self-driven, regardless of where the original idea to do the negotiation in the first place comes from. They are also typically competitive – they want to win, they want to be seen to do well. This doesn't mean they will win at any price, nor does it mean they won't concentrate on developing long-term profitable relationships, but they do have a strong set of internal standards which they want to see upheld. Interestingly, accomplished negotiators are often competing with themselves, rather than others – seeking to achieve against an internal, rather than an external, benchmark. When you think about this, what it means is that a good negotiator will have a very clear internally-focused reason for why they want to succeed in the negotiation.

But what if the purpose and outcome of the negotiation is determined by somebody else – typically, in a corporate environment, your boss, or the Board, or another department? And, even more significantly, what if you don't agree with what you are being asked to do?

In this situation, as in any other, there are only ever three things you can do:

- Do nothing;
- Do something; or
- Do something else.

Under these broad headings, some possibility thinking will help you to identify the consequences of these choices. This will help you find a strong Reason Why you want to go into this negotiation – remember – don't go into a negotiation without one; you'll soon be found out, and it will detrimentally impact your likelihood of success.

**"It is in your moments of decision that
your destiny is shaped."
Anthony Robbins**

When might doing nothing be the best outcome? By doing nothing, we mean not going into the negotiation – clearly there would still be a need to do something about explaining why you believe this to be the best option.

46

Doing nothing might be the best option if:

*   You are being asked to negotiate something which you know is absolutely non-negotiable from the other side. However, this comes with a health warning – is it genuinely non-negotiable, or do you just think it is? Many things that appear non-negotiable actually are – maybe by linking achievement of your goal with something else, or changing the shape and value to each party of a potential deal, or even by just waiting. Things that were absolutely not negotiable yesterday may be negotiable tomorrow. Things change. People change. Opinions and beliefs change. New options arise. New possibilities emerge.
*   What you are being asked to negotiate is not in the interests of the business you represent. Articulate why.
*   What you are being asked to negotiate is against company policy. But consider whether the policy should change. What is the policy there to achieve? Is it still valid for the business? Find out who 'owns' the policy and enlist their support for your position, or change theirs and move into the negotiation.
*   What you are being asked to negotiate is in conflict with what you stand for. This is tricky – why is there conflict, and what, or who, is causing it? Can that conflict be resolved in another way? Are you misunderstanding something? Is there another way around the issue – can the negotiating brief be changed to accommodate your personal value set? If no, then it's time to consider whether you are in the right place.

Entering a negotiation might not be the best option.

Doing something means getting on with it. Typically, your Reason Why in these circumstances will be influenced by the pressure on you, and it's a perfectly valid Reason Why to do something to relieve that pressure. A pragmatic negotiator will recognise when it is sensible and appropriate to pursue an outcome even if it's against their better judgement. Pragmatism is another perfectly acceptable Reason Why.

Doing something else opens up all sorts of possibilities:

Think possibilities.

- Influence whoever needs to be influenced to change the requirement;
- Enlist support from wherever it can be enlisted;
- Talk informally to the people you will be negotiating with – some intelligent, well-placed feedback about what the impact of formal negotiations might be can be extremely powerful in influencing the thinking of your own people to an alternative point of view;
- Think about other options that might be played in to great effect, seeking to add value to the whole process by ensuring that your ideas are workable and solution focused.

The wider your thinking becomes, the more likely it is that your opinion will be sought by those who set your mandate, and the less likely you will be placed in a position to negotiate something you don't believe in. This becomes a virtuous circle – as your experience increases, so too does your value to those you work with.

15. Defining your goals

Great negotiators know what their goals are. Goals need to be clearly articulated, and preferably written.

**"Man is a goal seeking animal.
His life only has meaning if he is reaching
and striving for his goals."
Aristotle**

As we have seen, there are three elements to the internal triangle in the Go MAD Thinking System – Reason Why, Self-Belief, and Defined Goals. Each are linked, and support each other to increase your probability of success. If you have a strong enough Reason Why you want to achieve something, you must Define your Goal. Then check your level of Self-Belief to ensure that you feel you will be able to achieve your Goal. We'll look at the 'how' later; for the moment, we are concerned with the 'what'.

A negotiating outcome, goal, or objective for commercial negotiations, is often set out in a negotiating mandate; this will often be a written document setting out, in effect, the instructions to the negotiator. Often, the negotiator has been pivotal in driving the creation of the negotiating mandate, although sometimes – and particularly in corporate life – the mandate is driven by others. In these circumstances, the negotiator may not have had a direct, or even indirect, input into defining what the negotiating outcome should be.

What is my negotiating mandate?

We have seen the importance of refining your Reason Why, regardless of whether the negotiating output originates from you, or from somebody else.

Surprisingly, all too many negotiating mandates are vague, non-specific, ambiguous and open to a number of different interpretations. This is of little use to the professional negotiator.

Therefore, before setting out on a negotiation, which will take time, effort, and money, the experienced negotiator will ensure that proper attention has been paid to ensuring that the negotiating mandate is clear, unambiguous, and achievable.

How clear is it?

Ways to express your goal

Clarity of goal defining is vital. If you have no goal, how do you know when you have achieved success? Perhaps even more importantly, how can you expect other people to know when you have succeeded?

In negotiations, there are many complex pressures that will conspire to draw you away from your goal, perhaps into an area or direction that appears more attractive, or easier to achieve. Only if you have clearly set out your goal will you be able to ensure that you stick to it, by checking your progress against your goal at regular intervals.

The most common way to express your goal is to set it out as a SMART goal. Like any other objective in life, a negotiating mandate can be formed in a SMART way:

- Specific
- Measurable
- Achievable
- Relevant, and
- Timebound

We'll look at the use of SMART goals in negotiations in a moment. First, however, let's look at another form of goal defining:

An umbrella goal is an overarching goal that can cover a wide area. For example, a corporate umbrella goal might typically be: "To grow profitability by 20% over two years whilst increasing market share to 12%." In business, umbrella goals are often referred to as Strategies – the big picture of where the company wants to be at a particular point, and how that achievement is going to be measured.

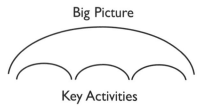

Umbrella goals

Big Picture

Key Activities

As with a SMART goal, this umbrella goal is clear in what it says, and in terms of what needs to be achieved and over what timeframe. It does not, however, address how this is to be achieved. The impact of this umbrella goal on your individual negotiations may, however, be significant. You may be required to drive harder bargains to improve profitability, whilst working to grow market share – two objectives which at first glance may look to be in conflict, but which require a coordinated approach to achieve. Equally, below the umbrella goal may be a range of other activities which make your job as a negotiator easier but are outside your area of responsibility:

It's important to see the big picture.

• The operations people may have been charged to reduce production costs so that you can pass cost savings on to your customers, and grow market share whilst winning deals that improve profitability;
• The logistics people may have been asked to do the same – distribution costs all have to be absorbed somewhere in your deals.

An umbrella goal which overarches the requirements placed upon you is fine, but for the purposes of setting a negotiating mandate against which your achievements can be measured – and your successes celebrated – it needs to be more specific. This is where SMART goals come into their own.

"People with goals succeed because they know where they are going."
Earl Nightingale

If a negotiating goal is not SMART, it needs to be developed. There are two key reasons for this:

• First, the mandate defines what it is that needs to be achieved, and if it is unclear in any way, then any preparation to achieve an unclear goal, and any time and effort put in to achieve it, may well be wasted. As the saying goes, if your goal is unclear, any road will take you there;

• Second, your achievements are going to be measured against the terms set out in the negotiating mandate. If those terms are unclear in any way, how do you know if you are doing the right thing and, if you manage to close a deal, what if any people to whom you are responsible thought that you were out to achieve something different? Not a good end to that particular day!

You can only ever celebrate success if you are truly, personally, proud of what you have achieved – and that means having a very clear definition of what you want to achieve, and then achieving it. And you should always plan how you are going to celebrate your successes as part of the planning for any negotiation – so your team, and you, are envisaging success and what will flow from that. This channels positive thought and energy. This is why sales incentive schemes state up front what will be paid for certain specified outcomes, or why football teams are told what the winners bonus is in cup competitions – the more people envisage what success looks like for them personally, the more they are going to focus on what they need to do to take them there.

What does success look like?

16. Checking your self-belief

The third element of the Go MAD internal triangle – together with your Reason Why and your Defined Goal(s) - is Self-Belief. When you go into a negotiation you should let your strong Self-Belief walk in with you – everyone will see it; this helps to establish your position on your own team, and will influence the people on the other side of your negotiation.

Great negotiators know how to recognise the level of their own self-belief, and know how to increase it to maximise their level of success. Note that we do not say 'chances of success' – accomplished negotiators do not leave anything to chance. That's for gamblers, where you accept that you'll win some and lose some. We're only interested in winning; every time, without fail.

Assessing your Self-Belief is straightforward: on a scale of 1 to 10, 1 being no belief whatsoever in your ability to succeed in this negotiation, and 10 being an unshakeable belief that you can deliver exactly what you want. If you score 5 or below, ask yourself what is causing this score. If you do not believe your goal is achievable, you may need to revisit your goal.

How strong is my self-belief that I can achieve my goal?

What if the goal is properly set out, in a SMART way, but you think there is something wrong with it? For instance, you look at what it is that you are required to achieve, but you do not believe it to be achievable?

For example, you are required to achieve a sale price for your product that is substantially above prices currently being paid in the market, and you have no advantages over your competitors in terms of quality, speed to market, brand, or the current level of advertising.

At the extreme, this can impact your level of Self-Belief, and make you question what you are there for. And we have already seen that you should not go into a negotiation with a weak (or no) Reason Why, and a level of Self-Belief that is lower than 6 out of 10.

The most obvious thing to do is to redefine the goal into something that feels more achievable. However, this might not be the right solution and, if your goal is set by someone else, it might not be an option. Faced with the

What to do when goals are imposed.

situation of an apparently unachievable goal, it is always worthwhile to follow these steps:

1. Carry out a possibility thinking (see chapter 20) exercise involving those on your side with an interest in the outcome of the negotiation. There may be some opportunities that you have overlooked which, if explored, make an apparently unattainable goal become attainable.

2. Consider whether your preparation has been sufficiently thorough. Do you have all the information you could possibly need at your fingertips? Do you have a thorough understanding of your own team's capabilities? – Are there skills available to you which will improve your chances of success? What do you know about the people you will be negotiating against? – How could you find out more, from people you know who have dealt with them previously? If you have an established relationship with the other negotiator already, what positioning might you possibly carry out which could improve your chances of success?

3. Look at your own Reason Why. Use the hints and tips in the Reason Why section to see if you can strengthen yours.

4. Having taken the three steps above, consider any degree to which your Self-Belief has strengthened. If your self-belief is still low, answer the question, "What is the cause?"

5. If the only answer to this question is that the goal is still unachievable, then there are two solutions available to you:

• Change the goal. This may well involve influencing others to change the goal, which is a negotiation in its own right, and you should therefore prepare for that negotiation as seriously and as fully as you would prepare for any other;

- Seek to achieve the unachievable. Sometimes there is no other viable option. You might succeed! However, on carrying out the negotiation, once you get to the point that is as close to your bottom line position as you can get, go back to the people who set your mandate and tell them where you can achieve a settlement at. It's for them to then consider whether this is good enough, or whether you should walk away from the deal. It's good business practice to walk away with the permission of someone else. It makes the wash-up discussions so much easier – you achieved what you could, and offered to settle at the most appropriate position available.

Most of the time that isn't necessary. The more experienced you are as a negotiator, the more people will seek your opinion when the goals are under consideration, and the more opportunity you have to influence those goals to something you know is achievable. This becomes a virtuous circle.

"The confidence of today can often be hidden by the imagined fears of tomorrow."
Andy Gilbert

Let's spend a moment looking at how time pressure can impact Self-Belief. It is quite usual for negotiations to take place against some timetable, or deadline. For instance, a negotiation between a buyer and a seller for a product to be stocked by a retailer needs to be achieved in time to meet delivery timetables. This might involve some quite complex logistics including manufacture – maybe overseas, distribution, and onward delivery. So, you're in a negotiation, discussing the price, and the other side says, "We're interested in taking 10, 000 units, our bottom line price is £3 per unit, provided you can deliver in 21 days because we'll be building a special promotion around this product if we decide to go ahead".

Example: Handling time pressures when negotiating.

You know it normally takes 28 days to organise delivery, but you've cut all the corners off before and achieved delivery in 21 days – just – and you know what your stress levels were like at the time!

The snag with this deal is that your bottom line price is £3.25 a unit, and for an order of 10,000 you can't go any lower.

How is your self-belief doing? Chances are, you are feeling that this deal will not come together because time is against you. Time, it would appear, is the enemy here, and in your mind are thoughts that if only you had more time you could do a better deal; you could persuade them to go for £3.25 a unit, or to order 15,000 units which might enable you to get closer to their so-called bottom line of £3 a unit. The clock, your diary, and the speed the planet orbits the sun are all conspiring to stop you getting this deal!

Only they're not, are they? This is a classic negotiating situation where two things are happening. Firstly, the people you are negotiating with are using time as a weapon to influence your thinking, and secondly, you are putting yourself under immense pressure as you think of all the problems that this time pressure is causing you. And this is playing havoc with your self-belief.

An enabling belief!

We will look at Possibility Thinking later, which is an extremely powerful tool for freeing your mind of clutter in all sorts of situations, including high pressure situations like this, enabling you to think of options which will lead you to a solution. At this point, however, suspend any disbelief you may have, and accept if you will that the following adage is always true: **"There is nothing that cannot be turned to advantage."** If this is true, then this situation can be turned to advantage.

How?

Let's look at how we might turn the time pressure back on the other side.

They've told you they are planning on running a special promotion. They have probably got a lot riding on this – they'll have done their planning work, calculated what profit they expect to make and what the contribution towards their cashflow is of their planned sales and, importantly, if they are expecting this promotion to launch in three weeks, they may well not have an alternative option ready to go if they don't secure your product. What this all means is that the other party should be the people who are feeling the time pressure, not you. We only need to find a way to turn the pressure back on the other side.

The following might do it: "I can guarantee delivery in 21 days – it'll be really tight, so I'll need to know in 24 hours. However, I can't go below £3.35 a unit for an order of 10,000. But I can do £3.25 for 15,000 units."

This is opening up possibilities as the negotiation is brought to a close – there's still some discussion to be had on the price, and perhaps even the quantity of the order, but the key movement is that the time pressure has now been pretty much moved to the other side. They are the people who need to make a decision against the clock. You have told them, in effect, that you can meet their timeframe, but only if the price is right. Thus, you are strengthening your position, and weakening theirs.

Think again about your level of self-belief; it is likely to have risen a few points. And if you can use this tactic once, you can use it again and again. Ask yourself what it is that is diminishing your self-belief, and then turn it round. There really is nothing that cannot be turned to advantage in the world of negotiating!

**"There's nothing you can do
that can't be done."
The Beatles**

---

17. Building your self-belief

If your level of Self-Belief in achieving your goals is lower than it needs to be, then there are some practical things you can do to help increase it:

- Ensure your preparations are as full as they can be. Do you have all the information at your fingertips that you would like?
- Are your team members all similarly prepared? How well do they know each other? Have they worked effectively together? Do you need to do any team building? Do you need to clarify their roles and responsibilities? Are there any conflicts on the team that need to be resolved? Do you have the right people on the team – do you need to add anyone in, or take anyone out of the team?
- Have you done your homework on the people you are negotiating with? What do you know about them? What do you know about what is important to them?
- Have you been in contact with people you know, or can get hold of, who have dealt with the other side before?
- Is your negotiating mandate clear? Are the people on your own side who need to give you permission or support all aligned, or do you need to do more work on this?
- Do you feel you have the right skills to progress this negotiation, both from your own point of view, and in respect of those on your team? If not, where are the gaps, and what can you do to fill them?
- Are any time pressures working to your advantage, or are they working against you?

58

If you have answered positively to all the questions – Wow! And well done. If not, you might find it helpful to do some more preparation.

18. Helpful and hindering thoughts – the four thinking components

Your Self-Belief is impacted by the thoughts that go through your head. When you think to yourself, your thoughts will either help or hinder your progress towards your defined goal. Your thinking is comprised of various elements which combine in a sequence unique to your experience and view of the world. We refer to these as the Four Go MAD Thinking Components i.e. the four things which you do in your head that most help or hinder your ability to negotiate and achieve results. These are equally as important as the Seven Go MAD Key Principles and crucial to understand if you are seeking to develop your negotiating ability.

In simple terms your thoughts are comprised of two elements – what you say to yourself and what you focus on. When you talk to yourself (inside your head) you will either be asking yourself questions, or making statements to yourself, and these questions or statements will either help you, or hinder you:

"How can I possibly succeed in this negotiation given all the pressures I'm under?" is a hindering question. More helpful is, "What could I do to ensure I succeed?" A hindering statement might be, "People are going to find out I can't do this". More helpful would be, "I can do this, just consider possibilities and then decide".

What am I thinking right now? Is it helpful or hindering?

The statements you make to yourself are most likely to relate to three things: you and your ability; other people and how they affect you; and the situation or environment.

"Whether you believe you can or you can't, you are right."
Henry Ford

When thinking, your focus will either be on the past, for instance recalling a past success (helpful) or an unpleasant memory (hindering), or on the future – perhaps imagining a positive and pleasing outcome (helpful) or things going wrong (hindering).

So, in no particular order, the Four Go MAD Thinking Components are:

1.   Statements you make to yourself about yourself, others, and/or the situation around you;
2.   Questions you ask yourself;
3.   Memories of the past you recall;
4.   Future outcomes you imagine.

By recognising these Four Thinking Components, you can start to notice which thoughts are helpful, and which are hindering – and then choose to develop your thinking in a more helpful direction to influence the likelihood of your success.

Important to remember these four components.

When negotiating as part of a team, it is useful to identify any hindering thoughts of your colleagues during the preparation phase. The simple, yet powerful, question, "What's going through your mind?" will elicit clues about which thinking component is prominent. For example, "I can't see how they are going to shift their position," is a hindering statement about the imagined future. A more helpful option would be a question, "What could I possibly do to ensure it will be easy for them to shift their negotiating position?" Notice how a change in thinking is likely to lead to different results. Later we will consider

What is the most helpful question I could ask myself?

how to use the four thinking components to our advantage during the negotiation.

19. Thinking about your thinking

Start to become consciously aware of your thoughts and how they impact your actions and behaviour. This is easily done by asking yourself the following questions:

*   What am I thinking?
*   Is it helpful or hindering?
*   What could possibly be more helpful?

Let's consider a couple of scenarios:

Imagine you are walking into a major negotiation. In this sense, 'major' means its outcome is important to you, for whatever reason. You have therefore done your preparation. Your team, if you have one, know the roles they will play. You have all the information you could possibly need at your fingertips – in your head, in documents, on your PC, or in the heads of people who are with you. You have worked through all the issues that might possibly come up. If anything truly unexpected comes up, you are confident that you can get an answer promptly. Your self-belief is high.

Then something ridiculous happens. Just as you are about to go into the room, someone hands you a piece of paper. On it is written, "Sorry about the short notice, but the finance director is stuck at the airport and you need to lead a negotiation in the other meeting room to convince the external auditors that we are complying with all relevant accounting conventions. Otherwise they won't agree the report and accounts. And, by the way, you've got an hour".

How would you feel at that point? Unless you have the necessary financial knowledge, the chances are you might be having some hindering thoughts. "That's not my subject, I don't know where to start. Who are these people? My team don't know anything about that!"

Think about your thinking. Whilst you would not choose to put yourself in that position, what could you say to yourself or focus on that would be most helpful? Control your thinking by changing hindering thoughts into more helpful ones.

**"We are what we think we are.
All that we are arises with our thoughts.
With our thoughts we make our world."
Buddha**

Now imagine a scenario where you need to negotiate something with somebody and you schedule in the time to do your preparation, talk to those people on your side you might need information from, prepare any presentational material and the like. The meeting is in the diary and is two weeks away. You haven't really started your preparation but you are very confident that everything will be completed on time for the negotiation meeting. You then get a phone call from the lead player on the other team who says, "We need to bring this negotiation forward. Your office said you've got a free diary this afternoon so if it's okay we'll come over now".

Would you go ahead with the meeting? Depending on your relationship with the other key player, you might decline, or possibly agree to meet, but on a limited basis – perhaps to hear what they have to say, or to better understand why this is suddenly more urgent. But you're not going to go into a negotiation cold, and with no preparation.

Back in the real world, pressures of all kinds invite us to take decisions about how we are going to spend our time — and preparing for meetings can all too often get squeezed out. There is a belief-system in many corporate environments that if you aren't meeting someone, or writing something, then you're not delivering. This is sometimes referred to as 'output phobia' — if you can't actually see or touch something that has been produced, then nothing has been produced. So, you can witness someone talking on the phone, or typing at a PC, or in a meeting room — they are clearly 'doing something'. However, someone sitting at a desk, without even a pencil in their hand, is often perceived as 'doing nothing'.

What if, however, the person sitting at the desk thinking (and they've been doing this for half an hour) is actually about to hit on a way to make an already good negotiating outcome great? Say by selling twice as much product, or increasing the profit margin, or saving cost? That's an output, but until it's realised, you can't actually see it.

How much time do I allocate for my thinking?

This belief-system is not helpful. It forces us to avoid activity which does not subconsciously look like work — even though it is. Think about your thinking.

20. Possibility thinking

How, then, can Possibility Thinking help us in preparing for a negotiation?

Experienced Go MAD practitioners will recognise that there are a number of questions we can ask ourselves in relation to any planned activity which will help us to think of potential issues which may arise. If used as part of a team activity in preparation for the negotiation, it is a good discipline to invite all participants to spend 10 minutes thinking through answers to these questions from an individual perspective. At this stage, no idea is a bad idea – no matter how off the wall it may appear.

10 possibility thinking areas to explore.

1. What possible tasks or things could help you in achieving your desired negotiating outcome?
2. What possible resources might be useful?
3. What possible reasons are there to involve others?
4. Who could possibly help you?
5. How could you communicate your goal to them?
6. How could you possibly obtain their help and get them committed to helping you?
7. What possible obstacles might you encounter?
8. What possible risks or implications might there be in pursuing your goal?
9. How could you possibly overcome these obstacles and minimise any risks?
10. What assumptions might you be making?

This activity is about increasing the level of thinking that happens before the commencement of the negotiation, to give you more options to choose from. Having a high number of options at your disposal clearly improves the likelihood of a successful outcome, and equally significantly, places more options at your disposal than those you are negotiating against.

These 10 areas should produce, between them, anything from 50 to 100 thoughts individually; and as part of a team thinking exercise, anything from 300 upwards.

A useful aid to getting your mind thinking about possibilities is to use a bubble diagram. This is simply a sheet of paper with the 10 possibility thinking areas, each contained within a bubble or circle. Write at the top of the piece of paper the issue or problem you want to think about, and then scribble down any thought that comes in to your head, prompted by what you see on the piece of paper in front of you. Tackle the bubbles in any order, and write what you think in any order. Go back to other bubbles when you have a thought that is relevant to that area. The purpose of this exercise is simply to capture thoughts, NOT to evaluate them at this stage – quantity is more important than quality. Even thoughts that may appear at first glance impractical, or even daft, may lead you, subconsciously, to the solution.

**"The way to get good ideas is to get lots of ideas
and throw the bad ones away."
Linus Pauling**

Once you have spent five or ten minutes writing down your thoughts, put them into a more logical sequence, and pull out the ones that appear helpful, and which might lead you to a solution or a way forward. Prioritise the top two or three; these are where you should focus your primary effort as you get into the detail of your preparations.

Before we look at each area in a little more detail, consider whether you routinely put this level of effort into your preparations. If you do, you will know that this places you at a substantial advantage as you go into a negotiation – because often you will be faced by people who, because of time pressures and personal choices they have made, did not prepare as well as you. And what about the rest of your team – are they preparing as well as they might? Diary it in – if it's in the diary, in writing, it's more likely to happen.

The following are some hints to start the creative juices flowing. However, your own ideas, in the context of the issues you face, are what are most important:

What possible tasks or things could help you in achieving your desired negotiating outcome?

- Is your negotiating mandate (your desired end result) clear and written down?
- Are the logistical arrangements for the meeting finalised (teas, coffees, lunches including if needed any special dietary requirements, the right size room, the right number of chairs)?
- Do all attendees know where they are going? Have you sent maps?
- Have you booked any parking spaces needed?
- Is there an agenda? Is everybody clear on what the meeting is all about?

What possible resources might be useful?

- Have you prepared any presentational material needed?
- Have you sourced the required presentation or recording equipment?
- Do you have hard copies to issue, and in sufficient numbers?
- Do you have examples of your product available, if appropriate?
- Have you access to any corporate hospitality that might help cement relationships?

What possible reasons are there to involve others?

- Have you got buy-in from those in positions of authority on your side?
- Have you got sufficient flexibility in your negotiating mandate from the decision-takers? If not, what further work is needed?
- Do you know the people on your own team?
- Do you know the people on the other team?

Who could possibly help you?

*   Are there people who can provide you with information that will help you in the negotiation?
*   Have you considered possible contribution by people you don't know, for example those who have dealt with similar situations or people, and to whom you could get access one way or another?
*   What about published articles on the internet or from specialist sources like Dun and Bradstreet, the TUC, trade organisations etc?

How could you communicate your goal to them?

*   Alongside a written negotiating mandate, have you arranged face to face discussions with key stakeholders, including those on whom you will rely to deliver the deal you reach?
*   How much, if any, of your goal might you usefully convey – perhaps informally – to the other side before commencement of formal negotiations?
*   Has your team got access to all the information they need?

Remember they are just possibilities to consider.

How could you possibly obtain their help and get them committed to helping you?

*   Have you discussed and rehearsed roles and responsibilities with your team?
*   Have you shared your thinking about tactics, and how you believe things will go?
*   Have you conveyed through what you have said, and the way that you have said it, that you have placed trust in your team members?
*   Have you brought everyone into the loop who might be able to help you as the negotiations progress, and have you explained how pivotal they are?

What possible obstacles might you encounter?

- Have you worked to identify everything that the other side may throw at you?
- Have you worked through scenarios from the most likely to the least likely?
- Have you considered what you might do if it looks as if no deal is achievable?
- What if the other side want to accelerate the timetable, but your side can't deliver any quicker – what will you do?
- What if the lunch doesn't arrive in the room when it's due – who will you involve to resolve it?

What possible risks or implications might there be in pursuing your goal?

- What if you simply can't get a deal at or above your bottom line?
- Can you afford to walk away with no deal?
- Will that detrimentally impact a long-term relationship? Has that been factored into the decision-taking? Can it be?
- If you agree a big deal, will that have detrimental impact on smaller, less valuable customers, and can you afford for that to happen?
- Are you putting too many of your eggs in one basket? What if you then lost the client?
- How might investors react if the share price plunged as a result of losing – or not gaining – a big contract?

How could you possibly overcome these obstacles and minimise any risks?

- What is the plan for addressing each of the possible problem areas you can identify?

What assumptions might you be making? What might you be taking for granted?

- Are you treating this deal as if it's in the bag, and becoming too complacent, perhaps because you have always succeeded with these people before? Nobody wants to feel that they are being taken for granted!
- Are you assuming that your team know what they are doing? Have you checked?
- Is a strong sense of self-belief based on a solid foundation, or is it arrogance?
- Is the other team going to be the same as it always has been, or is there a new player who you haven't found out about?
- What hindering thoughts might you, your team or the other team have?

These hints are by no means comprehensive; some will apply to all situations, and there are many other possibilities that will arise when you consider the particular circumstances you are facing. The key point is that the more work you do to identify the things that can go right, and wrong, and the greater the detail of work you do to address them, the greater your success will be.

**"Always plan ahead. It wasn't raining when
Noah built the ark."
Richard C. Cushing**

A final word in this section, and it's around assumptions: never assume that everything that people try to drill into you on management courses is good, valid input. At some time or another, someone in a position of authority comes out with that well-hackneyed phrase: 'Never assume. To assume is to make an ass of you and me'.

We prefer the more straightforward adage of 'challenge every assumption'. Applying this logically means that you can challenge the concept that assumptions are always bad. They are not. In particular, there is one assumption that you should always apply, without exception:

Always assume that your negotiating opponent is as smart as you are, is as well prepared as you are, and is spending every waking hour trying to get ahead of you.

The true saying should be 'to be complacent is to make an ass of you and me'. It's a shame it doesn't have a better ring to it, because it's better in every other respect.

21. Involving others

In the previous chapter we considered two particular questions around involving others: "What possible reasons are there for involving others?" and "Who could I possibly involve?"

There is an immensely practical reason for involving others in your preparations for a negotiation, and in the negotiation itself – it makes your job easier. Other people bring their skills, experience, and knowledge to the party. People with a positive outlook and an engaging personality bring energy to a situation: a 'can do' attitude can be as useful in a negotiation as a strong argument in favour of a particular course of action.

And beyond this, a negotiation is essentially a collaborative process – you will be negotiating with another team of people, whose opinions you are seeking to influence, and so in a very real sense you will be involving them as well. There can therefore be no negotiation without involving other people.

When thinking about ways in which you might involve other people, consider two further questions:

- What might they know that will help you with your negotiations?
- What might they be able to do which will help you achieve your goals?

People know things, and they know other people. In the preparation stage of your negotiation, we have seen how important it is to obtain all the facts and information that you might possibly need, and it is largely through other people that you will be able to assemble that database of knowledge.

"A single conversation across the table with a wise man is worth a month's study of books."
Chinese Proverb

Secondly, there are people who will know things about the people you are going to negotiate with – and if this is the first time you have negotiated with these people, the more that you can find out about them before the event, the better. Seek out people who have worked with members of the other team before, or who have intimate knowledge of this type of negotiation, or who know the industry sector that you will be dealing with. Even in terms of building relationships with the other team, it is useful to be able to pull on issues that are of interest to them, and show that you have an interest – and finding people who can help you with your preparation is time and effort well spent.

You also need to consider who you are going to involve directly in your negotiating team. Involve people who have particular areas of expertise; and people who already have established relationships with one or more of the people who will be across the table; and people who are quick at thinking on their feet, who you will be able to rely on to get negotiations moving again if they get bogged down.

Choosing the right people in your team is absolutely essential. Every member of the team should bring something important and valuable to the negotiation:

Choosing my negotiating team.

•   An ability to contribute to the discussion and debate by virtue of knowledge, experience, a positive personality, perhaps existing relationships with one or more people on the other team;
•   An ability to contribute to the implementation of whatever it is you agree in the negotiations – people who can see things through to a proper conclusion without the need for really close management are exceedingly useful;
•   An ability to help you get buy-in from others on your own side, through their visible support for you. 'Political' reasons for involving others are just as valid, and as useful, as any other reason.
•   A willingness to learn – and perhaps to lead future negotiations for you when their skills are at the right level.

Whoever you choose, it is the responsibility of the lead negotiator to ensure that they are properly prepared, that they fully understand the negotiating brief, and that they both understand, and are comfortable with, their role during the negotiation. Always ensure the team is kept up to date with developments – things do change in business as in all walks of life, and you don't want someone coming into the negotiation ready to sing off last week's hymn sheet if things have changed in the meantime.

Consider not just who to involve, but when to involve them. Involving people at every stage of your negotiations,

72

from preparation through the negotiations themselves, and at the right time, can reap significant rewards. Better to get people on your side early than late.

And don't overlook the benefit of involving people on the other team right up front – some prepositioning questions, asked informally before the negotiation even starts – can be immensely useful in helping you understand what you might need to do to get a deal, and to highlight particular areas of interest to them, and to you, which will make the negotiations themselves proceed more smoothly.

What informal prepositioning might help the negotiation?

22. Planning priorities

Having done your initial possibility thinking and explored the 10 areas outlined in chapter 20, including involving others, you should now be able to identify your key priorities for further planning. Very simply, there is the need to consider and decide:

*   What exactly will I do and by when?
*   Who will I involve and how?
*   How much time will I set aside to do these things?
*   How will I ensure that I spend the necessary time preparing for the negotiation?

Questions to focus the mind.

23. Planning to celebrate success

As well as planning the priorities in preparation for the negotiation, let's consider the benefits of planning to celebrate a successful outcome:

*   By planning how you are going to celebrate your success even before you start your negotiation, you are building a positive picture of achievement in your own mind and in the minds of the rest of your team.

- This builds self-belief, and engages the minds of your people on what needs to be done to achieve in the negotiation. This becomes palpable – and the team on the other side of the table will see this confidence as professionalism, and as a team who mean business. In itself, this contributes to the likelihood of your success;

- By celebrating your success after the event, you help build relationships within your own team, and this positions you well for your next success. Remember to include those people who have supported your team from the sidelines, perhaps with inputs to research, facts and information, and those who have been on standby to help address issues that might crop up in the negotiations. Each have helped contribute to the success of the negotiation, and are deserving of your recognition. And if you remember them, they'll go the extra mile for you next time.

Who should I include when celebrating success?

TIME TO CHECK

Ask yourself the following questions:

Am I clear about the Reason Why I am in this negotiation, and have I ensured my team are with me?

Is the negotiating mandate set out clearly, unambiguously and in writing? Has everyone who needs to support this goal given their agreement?

Have the team worked through the possibilities in preparation for the negotiation, and have we identified and agreed the priority areas?

Am I taking personal responsibility for the outcome of these negotiations?

Have I identified how the four thinking components are helping or hindering me and those involved?

Have I checked the level of my own self-belief, and that of the team? Have I taken appropriate steps to strengthen that belief wherever necessary?

24. Taking personal responsibility

There is only ever room for one lead negotiator on a team, and you need to be absolutely clear with yourself and with the rest of the team on who this is going to be. If not you, then who else?

If you are the leader of the negotiations then you have overall responsibility. You have been given the mandate, and may have been involved in negotiating and agreeing it. Certainly people will be looking to you to achieve it. So you must do the checks to ensure that your team are positioned to deliver – and this includes not just those who are going to support you in the negotiations themselves, but those on whom you will rely on to deliver what it is you agree at the end of the negotiations.

"What one does is what counts and not what one had the intentions of doing."
Pablo Picasso

Ultimately, taking personal responsibility is about articulating to yourself and others that the outcome of the negotiation is down to you. This is not about taking responsibility away from others. Think of your team as an orchestra, with you as the conductor. Each part of the orchestra has a role to play, and together you will create a symphony of success. But no matter how good each of the members of your team are at an individual level, without your leadership to bring them together as a team, and to drive their skills and abilities in the direction of your goal, they will not achieve the same success. This is a great responsibility – to take ownership of the success of your team – but it brings the greatest rewards in terms of personal achievement and satisfaction, as well as helping others to achieve at their greatest possible level of attainment.

Some people observe that taking this primary responsibility is a lonely job – but not if you involve others in the right way. Even though there's only one lead negotiator, it's a team game.

25. Parallel thinking – understanding the thinking of the other negotiators

We have looked at how you can use the strength and value of the Go MAD Thinking System to prepare you and your team for the negotiation. So far, we have applied this to your considerations, to your goals and to matters over which you have strong influence or control.

Less experienced negotiators will leave it there. So too will people who don't particularly like the preparation that is needed before starting the negotiation. However, there is a further stage in preparation which really sets great negotiators apart from average negotiators: this involves the ability to apply what you know not just to your own situation, but also to the situation the other side face.

"Seek first to understand then to be understood."
Stephen R. Covey

By definition, this is more difficult. You cannot know the position of the other side as well as you know your own circumstances. But you can use all of the information at your disposal, including:

- What you know
- Who you know, and
- What you might be able to find out

to envisage yourself in the shoes of others. Look at the negotiation from their frame of reference, as if you were really negotiating for their side against you, i.e. think as they would think.

Your considerations should be focused on facts that you think may be available to the other team, to issues which you think may be of importance or relevance to them, and to emotions you think they may be feeling.

Let's consider how the Go MAD Thinking approach we have used so far can also be applied to assist you in working out what might be going through the minds of those you will face across the negotiating table.

As part of your preparations use this check-list to help with your thinking.

1. Working out their goals and priorities
2. Knowing their reason why
3. Assessing their self-belief
4. Understanding who they are likely to involve
5. Identifying who has personal responsibility
6. Recognising the action they might need to take
7. Considering possibilities – what questions might they ask?

Thinking about what other people are thinking is sometimes referred to as Parallel Thinking – because you are thinking about other people at the same time as you are thinking about yourself and your own team.

Gaining competitive advantage.

By applying the above check-list, you are seeking to obtain an advantage in the negotiation. The more parallel thinking you do, the more likely it will be that you will consider the widest possible range of measures they might adopt. You will also profitably think of all the things that might be important to them, but perhaps less important to you – and vice versa. So, as the negotiations progress, you will be in a better position than them to take advantage of the situations and negotiating opportunities which will inevitably arise.

Furthermore, if you have worked with your team to 'second guess' what might come up in the negotiation, then you are putting yourself in the strongest possible position to consider how you might respond to things they may raise. So:

*   You have already decided what it is you want to do, in your initial preparations;
*   Now, you are beginning to think what it is you think they are going to do;
*   And this leads you to consider what you might do if they did these things.

Compare this to the negotiator who doesn't prepare anything – the ones who just go straight in, perhaps with a firm belief that they can blag their way to a result based on their past experience. You are actually three stages ahead of them. Do you consider that this is likely to put you in the strongest position, compared to them? Of course! Sure, they may get a deal without any preparation, but will this be the best deal they could have got? Most likely not.

"Success is dependent on effort."
Sophocles

It is immensely satisfying to do this work, and then to get into the negotiation and to find that the issues you thought the other negotiators would bring up are in fact brought up. In itself, this helps to build your own confidence and that of your team, which in turn will flow through into success.

Let's look at each area in more depth, using the techniques that we have already used in preparing our own position, but applying it to what we can reasonably expect to be in the minds of others.

26. Parallel thinking – working out their goals and priorities

*   What do you know about why they are here?
*   Knowing what you know about the people on their team, do they all share the same goal, or will different people have different goals?
*   What have you learned from any pre-discussions between your side and theirs? Have they actually told you what their true goal is or have they given you sufficient information for you to work it out?
*   Could they have said something to you, verbally or in writing, that is seeking to influence you to a particular understanding of what they are looking to achieve, and have they done this to help you, or to mislead you – for instance by seeking to downplay something that is actually really important to them?
*   What knowledge do you have about them, perhaps through earlier negotiations, or from people who know them or their organisation from previous experience? What does this tell you about what their goals might be?

What is their real goal?

27. Parallel thinking – knowing their reason why

- Why are they in this negotiation in the first place?
- Have they put themselves in the position of facing you across a negotiating table, or are they there because someone else has said so? Or because some external influence requires it, such as a change in the law?
- Have there been any changes in key people on their side recently, whether they are on the negotiating team or not? Could this impact, one way or another, the motivation of some or all of the people on the other team?
- When you get to meet them, plan to check whether they are all engaged in the discussion; what will you do if anybody is looking as if they have opted out, either from what they say and how they say it, or by being silent, or by giving off signs through their body language? How could you use this engagement, or disengagement, to your advantage?
- What will you do if they appear to have more than one Reason Why and, if so, how will you determine which appears to be the strongest and therefore the real reason why they are there?

28. Parallel thinking – assessing their self-belief

- What, if anything, do you already know about the level of their self-belief and what could you do before the negotiations start to find out more?
- How will you take advantage of the situation if their self-belief appears to be weak when you commence negotiations, and will this help or hinder you if a long-term profitable relationship with them is important to you?
- What will you do if their self-belief is extremely high, perhaps even to the degree that they simply expect you to agree with their proposals without any

Remember the four thinking components. What will they be saying, asking, recalling and imagining?

negotiation at all? How will you present your position in such a way that they become convinced that they have to negotiate properly?

29. Parallel thinking – understanding who they are likely to involve

- Who do you know that they know, and what might they have learned about you, your team, and your organisation, that might help them? How could you turn that situation to your advantage rather than theirs?
- What information might you expect them to have prepared? Look at this as if you were responsible for their preparations – what data would you want at your fingertips if you were them?
- What do you know about their ability to obtain information that they don't have, once the negotiations start? What support arrangements might they possibly have which they will rely upon to check information that you give to them? As a general principle, it is always sensible to assume that any factual information you provide will be subject to detailed scrutiny by them – and you don't therefore want to mislead them with false information because you will be found out. This would damage your negotiating integrity, and impact your negotiations detrimentally.

30. Parallel thinking – identifying who has personal responsibility

- What do you know, or what can you find out, about who has the real authority on the other side? What will you do if the authority figure is not actually on the negotiating team?
- What will you do if you find that there is someone on the opposite team who appears to have the authority,

and you don't know them or anything about them?
- What roles do you expect other people on their team to take?

31. Parallel thinking – recognising the action they might need to take

- How will you look out for things said or done that are vital to progressing the negotiation? (As distinct from things said because they feel they have to, perhaps to satisfy their wider audience – and which can therefore generally be disregarded.)
- Run through a full Possibility Thinking exercise to consider not what possibilities you have already worked on, but the possibilities you think they will have considered. Again, ask yourself what possibilities would you have come up with if you were leading their team rather than your own;
- And how will you respond to them? Are any in direct conflict with your own negotiating agenda, and if so, how will you respond if they come up? Assume they will, and be pleased if they don't!
- If you were them, what would your non-negotiables be? What would be your walk-away position?
- How badly do you think they need this deal, and how can you make that work to your advantage? If you don't think they need the deal particularly strongly, what steps might you take to strengthen their desire to reach an agreement with you, on terms that are mutually acceptable?

32. Parallel thinking – considering possibilities – what questions might they ask?

- Imagine that their team is sitting in a room, that they have as much information at their fingertips as you would wish to have if you were in their position, and

Parallel possibility thinking.

that they are thinking through the High Quality Questions that they are going to ask you. What are they and how will you respond?

- How will you turn any possible question to your advantage, by interpreting it in such a way that you take the negotiation in the direction you want, rather than the direction they want, whilst avoiding looking manipulative?

- What are the questions that you really don't want to be asked? There is a real temptation here to avoid this whole area, and hope it won't come up. Plan that it will – because if you haven't planned, you and your team could haemorrhage self-belief and confidence if it does. The other team will see this, and exploit it. So do the work in the safety of your own team. This can only benefit you.

How adequately prepared am I to deal with potential difficult issues?

As a final thought: just as you have now spent significant time and energy finalising your preparations through detailed parallel thinking, assume that the other team have done exactly the same thing. Never assume that you are better prepared than them. The true situation will become very obvious very quickly and, as we have already seen, the best prepared side has the greatest likelihood of success.

TIME TO CHECK

Consider the following questions:

> How could I most effectively research the people I will be negotiating with?
>
> How well do I understand the thinking of the other negotiators?
>
> When will I conduct a parallel thinking exercise and consider possibilities from their viewpoint?
>
> How could I involve my team in undertaking adequate mental rehearsal to handle any situation?

"An idealist believes the short run doesn't count.
A cynic believes the long run doesn't matter.
A realist believes that what is done or left undone in the short run
determines the long run."
Sidney J. Harris

PART THREE: THINKING DURING THE NEGOTIATION

33. Involving others to build great relationships

There is an old adage which says, "Build relationships whenever you have the opportunity, because when you need them you won't have time". Relationship building is simply another way of involving other people in helping you to achieve success, and this is never truer than in the world of negotiations.

Great relationships are built by individuals who understand and appreciate that negotiating is a collaborative art. When you know the people you are dealing with; when you know what they stand for and what is important to them; and when they know the same about you, then you are better placed to develop ideas and proposals which will be to your mutual advantage.

This doesn't mean you can't achieve great outcomes with people you know nothing about and have never met before – but the better your relationship, the easier it is for you to do business with them, and for them to do business with you.

The first step in considering how best to build an effective working relationship with the other party is to consider two important questions:

- Is the negotiation you are about to undertake a one-off, in which case the development of a long-term, mutually advantageous relationship is to a large extent unnecessary?
- Or is there any likelihood (no matter how remote) that you will have the opportunity to do business with these people again?

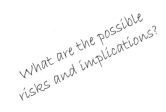

What are the possible risks and implications?

85

Whatever the answer to these questions, there are certain aspects which are common to both situations:

1. It's easier to reach agreement with people you like, and who like you;
2. Even if driving a particularly hard, one-off deal, you need to retain your personal negotiating integrity. It can be a small world sometimes, and people talk to people. If you take advantage of a one-off situation, bear in mind that it might come back to bite you – so don't risk your reputation amongst people who might do you damage if they are minded to;
3. We feel better about ourselves if we take the time and effort to ensure that everyone feels they have 'won' through the negotiation. Achievement of a 'win:win', even if the size of the win is weighted in your favour, is always worth it.

Win:win doesn't necessarily mean equal wins.

Let's take an example. Imagine for a moment that you are going round to view a house that you are interested in buying. The people who are selling the house are emigrating, and the likelihood is that you are never going to see them again once the transaction is completed.

Clearly you want to obtain the house at the cheapest possible price, and equally they want to sell it at the highest possible price. This may also apply to certain fixtures and fittings that are not included in the sale, but which might be obtained by separate negotiation.

What possible advantages can you think of to completing this transaction in a positive way, where the people you are buying off believe you have treated them fairly, even if firmly, and where they think they have obtained a reasonable price taking all factors of the deal into account?

And what if you have nailed them into the ground, as they see it? Does it matter, because you're never going to see or speak to them again? In fact, you may never have met them at all – the whole transaction, including the initial viewing, could have taken place through agents, solicitors, and advisers.

Put yourself in their shoes for a moment, and ask yourself this question – and remember, we are talking about human nature here, warts and all!

"The people buying my house are the worst people I have ever had to deal with. What can I do to make life difficult for them, without actually losing the transaction?"

This could develop into a lengthy list, but just to focus on a few irritating, or even quite costly, elements:

- Don't compromise on dates at all. Do what you want, especially if it makes things awkward for them;
- Remove fixtures and fittings, even if they are of no value to you, just to be awkward and to cause them more work, and additional cost when they move in;
- Don't leave the boiler instructions when you leave;
- Don't mow the lawn;
- Don't answer any follow-up questions once the transaction has been completed.

Could this and all the other niggling and annoying things that could happen, have been avoided either by being slightly more pleasant, or by not driving quite such a hard deal? Is what you could potentially get by driving the hardest deal possible actually worth the cost, both in tangible and intangible ways?

This is even more important when you are negotiating with people who either you will negotiate with again in the future, or indeed who may share their experiences – both good and bad – with others with whom you may, or already, negotiate. In such circumstances, great negotiators recognise the value in maintaining and strengthening personal relationships, to mutual advantage.

"Always do right – this will gratify some and astonish the rest."
Mark Twain

How you do this is an individual matter that is best rooted in whatever you are comfortable with. Some people value the opportunity both before and after negotiations to engage in social conversation with people from the other team. Some worry that they will let their guard down and give away vital information by accident – in fact, this only happens if you let it. At the end of the day, negotiation is a people business and we get to know people, and what makes them tick, by talking to them about our attitudes to things, how they feel, and by exploring areas of mutual interest. This can be achieved perfectly well whilst keeping things on a strictly professional level. Being professional doesn't mean you can't talk to people as people.

Of course we all have to deal with people who are difficult, or abrasive, and who are not interested in forming any kind of quality working relationship with us. In these circumstances, it's always advisable to work as hard as necessary to try to build an effective relationship, and to look for those qualities in the person that you like – there are very few people with absolutely no redeeming qualities whatsoever. In any event, developing the closest working relationship you can get in all of the circumstances is never wasted.

34. Using high quality questions to help your thinking

Our minds work most effectively when we are searching for answers. Some argue that all human progress is the result of a search for answers to huge questions like, "Why do I exist?" and, "What is the true meaning of life?"

It is even possible that you ask these questions of yourself in the middle of a negotiation that isn't quite going in the direction you had hoped! However, in most negotiations, the questions which will be of most use to you are a little more straightforward.

So what is a High Quality Question, which we'll refer to as an HQQ?

At its simplest level, an HQQ is a question which, if answered, will enable you to make progress. A well-designed HQQ will guide your thinking and the thinking of others to progress the negotiating discussion in the direction you want to go in, and to achieve the result you are seeking. The quality of the question you ask yourself will determine the quality of your thinking.

**"Learn from yesterday, live for today,
hope for tomorrow.
The important thing is not to stop questioning."
Albert Einstein**

---

35. Asking high quality questions to focus the mind

HQQs to focus the mind are a very effective way of getting to the heart of the detail. There are many circumstances in any negotiation where this is essential – perhaps to guide the conversation into a particular area, or to focus on deciding key elements of the potential deal.

Equally, HQQs can be used to check understanding of what you have already said, or elements of the discussion that have already been agreed.

Examples of this kind of HQQ include:

* "Would you run through the proposal in greater detail?"
* "What do we need to do to address this specific concern?"
* "What are the time-scales from order to delivery, so everyone is comfortable with the process?
* "Who is responsible for what?"
* "It's important that we capture the details of our agreement accurately, so are you comfortable with the following?"

36. Asking high quality questions to engage the imagination

HQQs designed to engage the imagination are usually possibility based and containing words like: possibly, could or might. They help people to think about the future without necessarily committing to a decision.

"The man who has no imagination has no wings."
Muhammad Ali

---

* "What if...?" For example, "What if we could guarantee a delivery time of 10 days? What impact could that have on your own delivery time, and cashflow?"

With this kind of question, you are prompting people to think beyond product quality and price. You are using a well-designed question to paint a picture in someone else's mind of other aspects of a potential deal which might be of benefit to them. You are also, very subtly, making a suggestion that they should start thinking about questions in their own mind which might help them to get more comfortable with your position, and possibly even to better sell the proposition to their own side.

- "What might be the response of your people if we were able to reach an industry-leading deal?"

Here, you are looking to stimulate thought about what success would feel like for them.

- "How might your company's reputation be improved through the establishment of a partnership with us?"

Again, you are seeking to prompt consideration of intangible benefits.

- "What are your holiday plans this year?"

A well-placed personal question which is about building personal relationships, and which helps to get a positive frame of mind – people usually like to discuss their holidays, and usually enjoy answering questions like this. Such a question might give the meeting a little time out from the intensity of discussion, or might be used to buy you a little thinking time, or even to change the mood of a meeting, perhaps if things have got a little heated.

37. Applying the four thinking components

During the negotiation you will be constantly thinking – hopefully helpful thoughts – inside your head. So now is the time to check each of the four thinking components:

- What am I saying to myself about my negotiating skills?
- What am I saying to myself about other people?
- What am I saying to myself about the negotiating situation or environment?

statements

91

- Are these statements helpful or hindering?
- What could I say to myself that is possibly more helpful?

questions

- What questions am I asking myself?
- Are these questions helpful or hindering my progress?
- What is the most helpful question I could ask myself?
- What is the most helpful question I could ask others?

recalled memories

- What aspects of the past am I focusing on?
- Are these helpful or hindering me in this negotiation?
- What is the most helpful thing I can recall to help me now?
- What can I learn from that experience? (Note: this is a particularly useful question to ask if you have had a recent experience that has not gone well and keeps popping into your head.)

imagined future

- What am I imagining the outcome of this negotiation to be?
- What am I imagining is about to happen?
- Is this helping or hindering me?
- What could I focus on that would be more helpful?

By asking yourself these questions, you are instantly influencing your thinking by controlling one of the four components in a helpful way. Thinking in questions is a technique that can be useful during moments of doubt or when hindering thoughts enter your head. Here is our favourite 'get out of jail' question for when the going gets tough and you need to interrupt your hindering thoughts:

- What is the most helpful question I can ask myself in order to move forward?

Notice that this a question purposefully asked in order to generate the real question that is most helpful for you at that particular moment in time. When you are consciously asking high quality questions to yourself in rapid succession in order to move forward it is virtually impossible to focus on hindering thoughts as your mind will automatically go searching for answers and solutions. On negotiating skills training programmes we refer to this as 'flooding' and help individuals develop the skill of asking rapid fire HQQs to themselves when under pressure. This really is the art of 'thinking on your feet' by consciously controlling your thoughts to ensure all four components are helpful.

Thinking on my feet by flooding the mind with HQQs.

" A prudent question is one-half of wisdom." Francis Bacon

In addition to focusing on the thoughts going through your head, you can also consider the current thinking components of the person, or team, you are negotiating with. A parallel thinking approach applying the four thinking components would involve asking the following questions to yourself as the negotiation progressed:

- What might they be saying to themselves about their position?
- What might they be saying to themselves about my/our position?
- What might they be saying to themselves about the current situation?
- Is it likely to be helpful or hindering?
- What do I want them to be saying to themselves?

statements

- What questions might they be asking themselves?
- What questions might they want answers to from me?
- What higher quality questions could I give them to think about?
- What might they be recalling from our past discussions? (Note: it is impossible to understand their

questions

recalled memories

imagined future

entire range of recalled memories, so focus on their possible recalled memories involving you or this negotiation, i.e. what happened earlier.)

• How could I possibly remind them of key points?
• What might they be imagining the way forward to be?
• What outcome are they imagining for themselves?
• Is this helpful or hindering for my desired outcome from this negotiation?
• How could I possibly help them to imagine an alternative way forward?

Remember that our definition of negotiating is, **'achieving results by influencing the thinking of others'**. In order to do this, we must first be aware of what the others are thinking and whether it is helpful or hindering. The four thinking components are our secret weapons and the most important of these is the ability to ask the highest quality questions to enable the highest quality thinking. The previous 31 questions provide a self-coaching toolkit to be used when negotiating.

Now, at this point, you might be thinking, "How will I remember or have time to do all of this whilst negotiating?" Well the key is to remember that when we think we are only really doing four things – talking to ourselves, asking questions, remembering the past and imagining the future. So what is the predominant thought? Is it helpful or hindering the negotiation? And, what can you do to influence it?

You have plenty of time to do this when negotiating because on average we speak at approximately 140 words per minute, in normal conversation (including pauses) yet have the capacity to think at approximately 500 words per minute. So what should you do with the remaining 360 words per minute? Give yourself the competitive thinking advantage by asking yourself great questions!

38. Responding to questions

As well as asking questions, you will be on the receiving end of them during the negotiation.

Be aware of the kind of questions you are being asked, their tone and content, and the way in which they are being asked. If you have been arguing over the price of 1000 units, and do not appear to have made progress, a question like, "So what would the cost of 2000 units be?" is very significant. It might be a signal that a bigger order is achievable, if the price is right. Or, it might be a tactic to get a lower price on the table, following which the other party could say, "If you can do that price for 1000 units we've got a deal". This opens up options for you:

1. *Could you do that price?* You may be able to close the negotiation now, and then profitably spend your time on other things.
2. *Could you do that price for 1500 units?* There may be opportunity to agree a sensible price, within your negotiating mandate, but actually to sell more units than you anticipated – a definite win.
3. *Could you do something in the middle, on price, quantity, or both?* There may be a flexible solution agreeable to both parties.
4. *What is most important to you?* If you are seeking to clear a warehouse to make room for incoming stock or materials, quantity sold might be more important than price. Re-examine your Reason Why and your Defined Goal.

Think possibilities.

Look for changes to questions as you reach closure in a negotiation:

- "How are we going to document a possible deal?" or
- "Could we potentially have this sewn up by the end of this week?"

These types of questions indicate that you are very near agreement.

Recognise the opportunity presented by a question which seeks to engage your imagination.

• "Hypothetically, what if we were to agree on the price and quantity we have discussed, and just get the delivery time down?"

A question that starts with 'hypothetically' is never a hypothetical question. This is simply another way of phrasing a 'What if...' question – it signals a potential move in the negotiation, and an invitation from the questioner to explore a potentially different outcome, or point of detail, which will lead to a point of agreement.

It can be very productive to answer a hypothetical question with another:

Recognise clues.

• "That wouldn't work. However, hypothetically, if we were to offer x, what would that look like for you?"

39. Handling telephone and video negotiations

It might seem obvious, but the only real difference between a telephone negotiation and a face to face negotiation is that one is over the telephone, and the other is face to face! The real issue, of course, is that in a telephone negotiation, you are denied the benefit of being able to read body language. Research studies have shown that 55% of a speaker's impact occurs at the non-verbal level – through poise and posture, facial expression, gestures, and other body language. Over the telephone, we can rely only on what is said, and the way it is said.

Observe the length of pauses in conversation during a face to face meeting: when you start to look at these things consciously, you find all sorts of interesting things:

- If you are talking to someone, and they take 9 seconds to respond, you probably won't even notice it as a pause;
- If you ask a question, and someone refers to their notes, a pause of 20 seconds is not unusual.

On the telephone, however, a pause of 9 seconds, never mind 20, seems like an age. We can't see what the person on the other end of the line is doing. We feel they may be stuck for something to say, or may be waiting for us to say something. These are assumptions that we make but which are not based on reality. The likelihood is that the person is simply thinking – but with no visual feedback we have no real way of telling – unless we wait for them to say something, and then respond accordingly at that point. We often feel that silences are there to be filled – fight the urge to say something else if the pressure is on the other person to respond. If they don't understand what you are getting at, they'll say.

If there is absolutely no response, a simple question to ensure that the person heard you in the first place is all that is required.

"If speaking is silver, then listening is gold."
Turkish proverb

A good negotiator learns to use the power of silence during negotiations – including those on the phone. It is surprising how much progress can be made by remaining silent; an inexperienced negotiator will often feel that it is their responsibility to end a silence, and may end up giving away facts and information which a more experienced negotiator would keep to themselves.

Be careful of what your silence might convey. It might be taken as a sign of aggression. You may use silence as a tactic to put pressure on the other side and vice-versa. If this is not the case then let them know you are going quiet to do some thinking or consider their point.

Be aware of different types of telephone negotiation. There are essentially two types: those where you know the person you are talking to, and those where you don't. If you do know the person, you will have experience of how they do business, what their personal style is, and what encourages them to react to you and your proposals well. However, recognise that some people have a different style on the phone than they do face to face. Some people can come across as more direct, less polite, or more pushy on the phone than in person – this is because they do not believe they have to deal with a negative reaction from you, or hostile body language. Therefore, you may need to be equally direct back. But take care to consider the possible risks and implications.

"It is easy to be brave from a safe distance."
Aesop

Imagine you are negotiating over the telephone with someone you don't know. Whilst you have no personal relationship with them, what do you know about them? What can you find out before you speak? Who do you know who has dealt with them, or their company, before, and how did it go?

Treat telephone negotiations with the same degree of care that you use in any other negotiation – the only difference is that you aren't together with the person or people you are talking to. Therefore, you aren't going to be able to use your own body language, or theirs, to emphasise your points or better understand theirs. So, you need to be particularly clear on what you say, and how you say it. In every other respect, it's the same thing – prepare, do your homework, and build your confidence by knowing your subject.

Recognise the benefits of sending written material or presentations to people you deal with over the phone: it can be extremely productive to talk people through a PowerPoint presentation in real time; this will help you to structure the conversation, and raise the issues, that are important to you.

Run conference calls with particular care; ensure you invite all participants in the call to take part, not just the ones who do the talking. Do everything possible to find out who the decision taker is before the call, and recognise that their opinion is vital, so seek to bring them into the conversation if they are not talking. Check their understanding of key issues through appropriate high quality questions.

What possible resources could help me achieve my goal?

Video conferences are actually nearer to a telephone call than to a face to face meeting. From an early age we watch television, and – whether we know it or not – we train ourselves NOT to take in a great deal of detail; in television programmes we will miss in excess of 80% of the information available.

It is exactly the same with video conferences: the sight of an individual or team of people, on essentially a small screen, does not convey body language in the same way as actually being there. Chemistry between human beings is, as we all know, an extremely complicated area, and chemistry does not come across through a video conference.

Once this is appreciated, the same ways to compensate through concentration on what is being said, and how it is said, applies.

99

40. Diagnosing potential problems

The final part of this section focuses on how you can use the Go MAD Thinking System as a diagnostic tool to help improve your ability to negotiate successfully.

We have already examined how you can use Go MAD to guide your own thinking, and to help understand the thinking of others. As we have seen, this is as useful during the preparation for the negotiation as it is in the negotiation itself.

But what if things are going wrong?

Picture yourself in the middle of a negotiation on a matter which is important to you, and imagine that things are not going your way. Progress is not being made; time is against you and it is increasingly looking as if no deal is going to be reached.

"In the middle of difficulty lies opportunity."
Albert Einstein

You may be able to use the following techniques yourself during the negotiating meeting. If this isn't appropriate for whatever reason, typically if you want to discuss matters with your team, then call an adjournment. You never need a reason to call an adjournment; simply say you need a natural break and a few minutes to review the situation with your team. No weakness is implied by doing this.

Using High Quality Questions – HQQs – focus your attention and that of your team to address each of the Go MAD Key Principles.

Consider each principle in relation to yourself. Ask yourself the question, "Where is the bottleneck? Or what is causing the problem?" Keep the language positive – even in your own head when you are thinking rather than talking out loud. Once you have identified where the blockage is you are then able to ask possibility questions to begin the process of progressing the negotiation. The following HQQs will help to focus your mind:

- How strong is my reason why?
- Do I still really want this deal, and if not, why not? What has changed?
- How strong is my self-belief? Has this changed, and if so, why?
- What information could I access which will help me feel more confident in this negotiation, and how might I possibly obtain it?
- Is my goal still clear, and is it still the right goal? Has anything changed, and if so, what and why? Has anything occurred which persuades me that the goal is now wrong, and if so what are the steps I need to take to adjust the position? Who else do I need to involve in this?
- Have I considered all the possible actions that I can take, including different approaches and negotiating tactics? What possible ways are there to overcome current hindering thoughts and other obstacles?
- Are my priorities clear? Are there other steps I should be taking? Should I seek to accelerate, or decelerate, the proceedings?
- In terms of others I am involving, have I got the right experience and knowledge available to me, either directly, or through my team? Are there other people I could call upon who might be able to assist me to break this deadlock?
- Am I taking all appropriate steps to assist the other side to see the benefits of my desired position? What else could I possibly do to engage their imagination to work towards my goal, whilst satisfying their own need for a successful outcome?

- Have I taken personal responsibility for driving this negotiation forward? Am I doing everything I possibly can to lead, or contribute to, my team's performance? What else could I possibly do in this regard?

If you identify areas that are weak, then you can move to a personal possibility thinking exercise to consider what other steps you could take to put matters right. If the negotiation is truly stuck, then taking the time out to apply yourself to this process will lose you absolutely nothing – because the negotiation was going nowhere anyway. Freeing yourself from the intensity of the negotiation, and buying yourself some time, can be an extremely liberating experience when it comes to improving your ability to think. And never underestimate your subconscious mind's ability to help you out simply by sleeping on the problem. Great negotiators recognise the benefit, in times of need, of 'sleeping on it'.

Having considered the above HQQs in relation to yourself, involve your team and put the same questions to them. Then, apply exactly the same process to what you know about, or believe to be the case in relation to the other side's thinking. Do they still appear to have a reason why they want this deal? Has it changed? What might you possibly do to increase their reason why? And so on.

"Do what you can,
with what you have,
where you are."
Theodore Roosevelt

One thing is certain. If things are not going well in a negotiation, something has to change, and there are only so many people who can possibly change things. Take personal responsibility and do it yourself – if your reason why is strong enough!

TIME TO CHECK

Having reached the end of this section, reflect upon your realisations and consider the following prompts:

Have I considered how I can strengthen personal relationships to help me arrive at a great outcome?

Have I developed a range of High Quality Questions which I and my team can use as the negotiations progress and to lead to successful closure?

If any of the negotiations – whether informal or formal – are going to take place over the telephone or by video conference, have I taken into account the differences in approach that will have to be taken?

Do I appreciate the positive ways in which the Go MAD Thinking System can be used as a diagnostic tool to keep the negotiations on track?

In closing the deal, have I ensured that the deal is properly documented, and that the understanding of all parties as to what has been achieved is the same?

"Let us never negotiate out of fear
but let us never fear to negotiate."
John F. Kennedy

PART FOUR: THINKING FOLLOWING THE NEGOTIATION

41. Assessing success and identifying key issues

The Go MAD Thinking System can also be used as a diagnostic tool after the negotiation is finished – but in this case, it is an extremely useful exercise to use these tools and techniques to examine what went right as well as what might have gone better. Everything is a learning experience – great negotiators will always take a little time, with themselves and with their teams, to look at what went well, so they can do more of it next time; and what went not so well, so you can work to improve.

Emotions tend to run high at the conclusion of a negotiation, regardless of whether you have achieved your goal or not – and the emotions will be related not just to the level of your success, but also to the kind of person you are. Different people react in different ways – some negotiators take a really positive attitude when a negotiation has not gone as well as they like, because they take this as a challenge to do better next time. Equally, some negotiators, after achieving a truly great deal, will be depressed for a couple of days, as the adrenalin goes out of their system and they experience anticlimax. It is important to be aware how you react to both success and failure, to recognise that reaction as normal, to live with it, and to appreciate that your team will need their own space to react in their own way.

Doing a few diagnostic checks immediately after a negotiation is concluded may well be appropriate – you are likely to have to convey the result of the negotiation to others who will be keen to know how you got on, and planning how you are going to approach this is as important as any other element of planning for negotiation. The important thing at this stage is the headlines:

105

- What was the result?
- What are the key features of the deal that has been reached?
- If no deal has been reached, what will happen next – are you in an adjournment, or have the parties agreed to keep the dialogue open if any new movement becomes possible from anyone?
- Or have talks broken down?

And if talks have broken down, how important is that to you? If important, what steps do you need to take in order to be able to reconvene?

"When defeat comes, accept it as a signal that your plans are not sound, rebuild those plans, set sail once more towards your coveted goal."
Napoleon Hill

The absolute best time to carry out this thinking is actually not when emotions are running at their highest – people think best when they are relatively calm and relaxed. However, time pressures don't always permit the luxury of relaxation and in such circumstances taking a systemic, procedural approach to the issues in hand ensures that nothing important is missed.

42. Applying the four thinking components

Let's assume that a negotiation has ended, that the parties have gone their separate ways, and that no deal has been reached. No agreement has even been reached to reconvene the discussions.

Consider the key thinking components in relation to your current circumstances:

- What questions could you ask which, if answered, would lead to an improvement in the situation?
- What statements are you making to yourself, and amongst your team, which are hindering progress?
- What statements could you make which will potentially help progress?
- What memories of success do you have? What experience do you have of getting out of situations like this one which, if repeated, will move you to a conclusion?
- When engaging your imagination, what possible vision of success can you see which will potentially help you to move forward?

questions

self-talk statements

recalled memories

imagined future

In this situation, there are two points to focus on initially:

1. What could possibly be done to every aspect of the discussions which would make the key aspects of the deal more attractive to each party? Consider what changes could be made to your position, and what changes could be made to their position, which might help. Consider other elements that can either be brought into the discussion, or indeed removed from the discussions, which could assist. Put yourself in the shoes of the other party and look at the blockages from their point of view – carry out possibility thinking to find ways of making the situation more attractive all-round.

2. How could the talks be reconvened? If there are no talks, there can be no deal. Consider the best way to achieve a recommencement of the discussions – perhaps the lead negotiators should have an off-line conversation, either face to face, or by telephone. Avoid going into writing if at all possible – whether by letter or email. This is because the ideas that can be sparked in conversation, and which can lead to a breakthrough where previously there was deadlock, happen best in conversation.

Further possibility thinking.

107

Then, in turn, consider each of the seven key principles within the Go MAD Thinking System.

"There is nothing which persevering effort and unceasing and diligent care cannot accomplish."
Seneca

Ultimately, if both parties have a strong enough reason why, these techniques will, when properly and carefully applied, lead to a breakthrough. Remember that negotiation is not over until it is truly over – so never give up!

TIME TO CHECK

Having reached the end of this section, reflect upon your realisations and consider the following prompts:

Have I taken the time to ensure all those people who now need to work to deliver the output of the deal know what they need to do, and by when?

Have I planned in time to learn the lessons at the end of the negotiations so that we can do more of the things that went well, and avoid the things that went less well, in future?

Have I organised something to celebrate our success? Have I thanked everyone who was involved, directly or indirectly?

Am I ready for the next negotiation challenge?

PART FIVE: QUESTIONS AND ANSWERS

This section sets out, in a clear and easy to follow format, a wide-range of questions which crop up at each of the three stages in a negotiation. Many of the questions were submitted as part of the research for this book, and reflect true-life concerns that people have already experienced.

Use this section firstly to consolidate the tools, techniques, hints and tips set out in Parts One-Four, and secondly to dip into as a reference source in times of need.

The answers given, whilst full, do not aim to repeat all of the information covered in Parts One-Four – so it is always useful to cross-reference back to earlier chapters for the fullest guidance in each particular area covered. Where you notice the answers containing the word 'I' instead of 'we' this is Jonathan sharing his insights and providing a personal perspective based upon his extensive negotiating experience.

Thinking ahead in negotiations

In this section we explore pragmatic solutions to issues which negotiators face in any situation, regardless of their level of experience. Building on the tools and techniques explored within Part One, we illustrate how these can be applied in a skilful and effective way to achieve great results.

Let us first look at questions which are relevant when you are thinking ahead about the negotiation. The key elements you need to consider are:

* Know your reason why and define your goals;
* Explore possibilities and plan your priorities;

• Consider the skills you need both in yourself and in those around you.

43. What makes a great negotiator?

That's what this book is about! Let's summarise the key personal qualities that you need to become a great negotiator:

• An understanding of the three stages of negotiation, and the tools and techniques which can be employed to maximise the likelihood of success;
• An understanding of how to get the best out of yourself, and your team;
• A keen interest in preparation prior to the negotiation, including parallel thinking to consider what the other team are thinking about in their preparations;
• An interest and understanding of how to build, maintain and improve relationships with those people who are important to reaching a deal;
• An ability to follow through, and deliver what has been promised;
• A developed sense of personal integrity, and an ability to convey, and build, trust;
• An ability to involve people who can contribute to the negotiating process.

How do I rate myself?

How would others rate me?

Great negotiators tend to be good communicators, although there is no particular advantage to being extrovert as opposed to introvert – the most important thing is to be able to clearly convey thoughts and ideas to move the negotiation forward. Great negotiators will also be able to separate the wheat from the chaff and focus on what is relevant. They will be calm under pressure, and will have the ability to be patient. They will also have a range of tools and techniques at their fingertips, together with a sense of which to use, and when.

110

The good news is that this can all be practised, and refined – as long as you have a strong enough Reason Why.

44. What leads people to become a negotiator in the first place?

This is a question we asked everyone who took part in the research, and perhaps not surprisingly everyone has a story to tell – there seems to be no particular common denominator for how people got into this field. For me (Jonathan), the answer is quite simple. In the late 1980's I was in a policy and project role within the Human Resources department of one of the UK's leading financial institutions, and my work often involved developing initiatives which would change core terms and conditions of employment. Working in a strongly unionised environment, many of these changes needed to be negotiated with unions, who were often opposed to change, either because they didn't like the proposals, or because they had a wider and sometimes political agenda. Early in my career I was given the opportunity to support these negotiations – actually starting out as the guy who took the minutes. I quickly realised that the cut and thrust of the negotiations, the excitement of getting a great result, and the challenge of influencing people in their point of view, was a really stimulating, and fun, thing to do. This desire to make a difference through influencing people in a wide-range of situations strongly influenced the direction for my career.

So I started out with relatively small negotiations, working with some excellent people who had a solid track record, and who I could learn so much from.

I developed my own style, as all negotiators do, largely by adapting tools and techniques that I admired in other people, and moulding them to my own style and personality. Some things I saw I didn't much like, so I didn't adopt them. And I found that once I had an established reputation as a successful negotiator with sometimes extremely difficult union situations, my skills came into great demand in a far wider range of commercial negotiations as well.

Always seek out the experienced negotiators and work with them, observing them and profile their thinking by asking them HQQs about the way they think in given situations before, during and after a negotiation.

45. Why is it important that a negotiator has to stand for something – to have a personal value set?

Our research in this field demonstrates that a successful negotiator has to stand for something. By that, we mean you have to have a core set of values so that other people know who you are and what you stand for. This doesn't mean a set of values drawn up, as is the case in so many organisations, by leaders who are seeking to communicate what an organisation stands for in the minds of its customers, and people who work there. We mean the core set of values that you personally stand for – what makes you tick. And to be an effective negotiator, you have to have honesty, tact, diplomacy, and integrity. If people don't trust you, you won't get the best deals. People who think you have let them down, or have been taken advantage of, will remember that for ever. Of course there are differences of approach in different situations – as we'll see later, there is a difference between a commercial deal with someone who you'll never see again – say if you are buying or selling a house – compared say to a long-term commercial relationship. But a negotiator who has no personal integrity has nothing.

What do I stand for?

"The ultimate measure of a man is not where he stands in moments of comfort, but where he stands at times of challenge and controversy."
Martin Luther King Jnr

It is easy to see integrity in people you admire. And I have seen people lose all personal credibility in the eyes of the people they negotiate with, and in the eyes of people on their own team, because they don't have it. I have never seen a truly successful negotiator over the long haul who has no personal integrity, and who does not build trust and rapport with people on the other side of the table.

46. But surely negotiation is all about lying – I mean if you are buying a car you might say you can't possibly afford the price, even though you can, so you get a better deal. So how does lying sit with personal integrity?

It's important to understand the difference between a negotiating position, and a downright lie. In negotiations, there are unwritten rules between experienced negotiators – so if you are negotiating a price on the sale of 10,000 widgets, you may say you can only sell at, say, £1 each. You know your bottom line is 80p a widget. If you can get your 80p, you're happy. Anything above 80p and you're ecstatic. Your buyer, on the other hand, will suspect that if you've offered to sell at £1, you'll probably go lower. But they won't know how much lower – that's where the negotiation comes in.

What is my opening negotiating position?

But what if you say, during the discussions, "I can go to 80p and this is on the basis that you take delivery in 10 days and pay 30 days after that" – but you know your widgets won't be manufactured for 3 weeks. That's a lie. Lies will come back and bite you, whereas a well thought out, and authorised, negotiating position won't.

So in these unwritten rules understood by experienced negotiators – the opening offer is rarely the final position; each individual, or team, are out to do the best they can and will reach the best outcome possible – bearing in mind that the best outcome is not always the best deal as measured in a financial sense. The best outcome might be short of what you would most like, but if a long-term, mutually advantageous relationship is strengthened, with the likelihood of repeat and profitable business, then this is well worth achieving. In the case of buying a car, which is probably a one-off transaction unless you are a fleet manager, you go for the best deal you can – and a negotiating position, honestly held, does not impact your personal integrity – nor the integrity of whoever you are negotiating with.

47. Are negotiations essentially always combative?

Helpful thinking!

It can look like that! However, all negotiations are aiming to achieve an agreement between the parties on something to be done, and all agreements are ultimately collaborative. Whilst the discussions themselves may be heated at times, each party is there to reach a conclusion, and whilst the power and influence of each party may well not be equal, each needs the other – otherwise you wouldn't all be there negotiating in the first place!

48. What then are the key skills you need to develop to become a good negotiator?

These are our top five tips for what makes a good negotiator, in no particular order:

First, you need a clear set of personal values, married to an ability to convey what those are. People need to know what you stand for as a person before they can learn to trust you. Trust is hard won and easily lost.

Second, you need to be a good communicator. It doesn't matter what your personal style is, whether you are introvert or extrovert, concise or flowery in your use of language, loud or quietly spoken – the point is, you need to be able to get your point across in a way that is clearly understood, and to be able to clearly understand what is being said to you. In a career as a negotiator, you will come across all sorts of people, with different styles, different personalities, different levels of intellect – but they are all there to do a job, and you need to both understand, and to be understood, in order to progress.

Third, and this isn't as obvious as it sounds, you need to be able to think in a solution focused way. We have looked in this book in some detail at how the Go MAD thinking System can be used to great effect through any negotiation:

- To guide your essential preparations before a negotiation starts;
- To help you during the critical phases as your negotiations progress;
- And to support you in closing the best available deal as the negotiations draw to a close.

Fourth, you need to be able to build and maintain good and effective relationships with people. In any negotiation, there are always going to be quite a few people you need to deal with – people on your side, perhaps senior people in your organisation who define what your negotiating parameters and outcomes are; people on your team who you need to be able to work effectively with; and of course the people who you are negotiating with. You very substantially increase your chances of success, and make your life so much easier, if you can develop and maintain good relationships both at an individual and a team level. Hans Blix, the former United Nations weapons inspector

How successful am I in building effective relationships?

115

in Iraq, said when asked about the issue of relationships between negotiators in difficult circumstances: "I liked the people I dealt with on a personal level, but this didn't mean I believed what they were saying."

It really does help if you genuinely like working with people. Negotiating is a people business – it's about influencing how people think and feel about something – whether you are a commercial negotiator, a union negotiator, or a hostage negotiator. Your purpose is to get people as close as you can to your point of view; and so if you are to influence people effectively, it is really helpful if you like working with people. This doesn't mean you have to agree with them, but it's about general mindset.

"It is our attitude at the beginning of a difficult undertaking which, more than anything else, will determine its successful outcome."
William James

And fifth, again linked to mindset, it really helps if you are a positive person. If you always go into negotiations expecting to fail, that – more often than not – is exactly what will happen. Failure in my view is failure not just to get the deal, but failure to get the best deal. The former is obvious for all to see – the latter less so. But that could cost you, or your organisation, considerable sums of money, business opportunity, market share, or reputation. So you have to believe in yourself.

49. What abilities do you most need to demonstrate to be a successful negotiator?

Three things are important, alongside the personal qualities we have already looked at:

- First, know your subject;
- Second, be absolutely clear on what your goal is, and stick to it;
- And third, appreciate the different phases in each negotiation, and how to handle each of them.

When I say you need to know your subject, I mean that you have to know what you are talking about. If you are negotiating a commercial deal, you need to do your homework so you know what is, and what is not, going to be acceptable to your side and to the people you are negotiating with.

Knowing your goal, and sticking to it, is vital. You need to be able to clearly articulate your goal for yourself, and for your own team – which means potentially negotiating with the people on your side who give you your negotiating mandate – you don't want to be saddled with an unachievable objective. By the same token, making a deal easy to achieve doesn't make it the best deal. You have to work hard to get great deals – and once you've got them, there is no harm in blowing your own trumpet a little so your own people know what you've achieved – especially if you have performance bonuses riding on the back of your achievements. So goals should be SMART – specific, measurable, achievable, relevant, and timebound.

There are three distinct phases in a negotiation:

- Before you start, where you need to think ahead about the negotiation;
- During the negotiation itself;
- And what you do after the negotiation is concluded.

The three stages of negotiation are explained in detail in earlier parts of this book.

50. Recognising that there are many different types of negotiating situation, ranging from commercial   deals to pay negotiations to hostage negotiations, to what degree do you believe the skills needed are different?

This is a question which featured strongly in the research. We spoke to a number of people from diverse backgrounds, to see what their views were. Our conclusions were clear; whilst the outcomes of different types of negotiations were extremely varied – you can hardly measure the success in saving someone's life through a hostage negotiation in the pure financial terms of some commercial negotiations – the skill set needed by the negotiators was identical:

What are my strengths?

- An ability to form a strong and trusting bond with the other side;
- A keen drive to prepare as much as possible in the circumstances, including getting to know as much as you can about who you are dealing with before you meet or talk to them;
- A clear negotiating goal;
- The ability to think on your feet and to react to unexpected and changing circumstances;
- An unshakeable self-belief, built on experience and on living the maxim that there is nothing that cannot be turned to advantage;
- The ability to disengage emotionally, at least to some degree, so that you can remain calm under intense pressure and sometimes startling provocation;
- A strong personal sense of ownership and accountability for the outcome of the negotiation;
- A keen competitive edge, often manifesting itself in a desire to do well against a personal, internal standard;
- Often, a sense of humour, generally as a safety valve for immense time or other pressures.

51. What is the best and most effective way to learn how to become a better negotiator?

There are three main ways to become a better negotiator:

*   To learn from research,
*   To learn from other negotiators,
*   To develop your skills by taking part in negotiations.

The Go MAD approach is a combination of these three. Our research gives fascinating insights into key questions that people who are interested in developing their skills have put to us. We have also tapped into the skills and knowledge of a broad range of accomplished negotiators who have been willing to share their experiences so that other people can develop their skills. And finally, our approach is to deliver these insights in clear, easily understood, and highly practical ways so that people can practise and refine their own skills in a live environment.

52. What many people find fascinating about negotiating is how much of it is shrouded in mystery. Why is this?

Often, commercial and other negotiations have a mystique about them – they appear to take place in secret, and are carried out by people who seem to understand a completely different language. This mystique is only added to when you look at the media portrayal of significant negotiations that go on late into the night. Just what, one wonders, are they up to?

In actual fact, the negotiators are most likely having a series of conversations with each other, whilst ensuring that their respective negotiating positions are kept a closely guarded secret – to reveal your hand to the other party is only going to weaken your position unless you are good and ready to reveal it.

How many times do we watch news reports say of negotiations to resolve a trade dispute either between an employer and a union, or between one country and another, or even peace negotiations – where the stakes can be immense, and measured in lives not money? And a spokesperson will appear to camera on some steps somewhere saying, "We have spent the day in useful and productive discussions and will be meeting again in the morning". This tells you absolutely nothing about what is going on. And the reason is simple – the spokesperson doesn't want the other party to be able to read anything into what's said. In actual fact, more often than not the parties will have agreed amongst themselves that each will say something equally non-committal if asked. Even seasoned journalists know not to push this one.

53. Do you have to be something special to successfully negotiate huge deals?

Every negotiation, at its core, is like every other, no matter how big or small.

Sound negotiating skills apply to every negotiating situation – buying or selling, tangible things or concepts, commercial deals or peace deals, it doesn't matter.

And we all negotiate, every day, in some way or other, whether we know it or not. Let's take the drive to work – this is a complex, non-verbal (or mainly non-verbal!) interaction between car drivers who are partly cooperating, and partly competing. You have to think quickly in potentially threatening situations, follow a certain set of rules and check to see that others are doing the same thing, whilst all the time staying one step ahead of what everyone else is doing or thinking. When you think about driving to work in this way, you appreciate that the core skills you need to be a successful negotiator are already there — you just have to learn to make better use of them.

**"Over the long run, superior performance
depends on superior learning."**
Peter Senge

---

54. What preparation is required?

Preparation is everything. The more you know about the issues on which you are negotiating, and the more you know about your own team and those on the other side of the table, the more confident you will be. If you are confident, this will show through in your negotiation. Confidence breeds self-belief, which flows through to achievement.

To achieve great results, there is no alternative to preparation. If there is no time to prepare, make time. It is better to use time to prepare than to waste time in a negotiation for which you have not prepared, and which will ultimately lead to a poor result, or maybe no result at all. Preparation saves you time, and makes you money. Preparation is not optional. All good negotiators know this, often having learned the hard way. Take the easy route — prepare!

Follow these straightforward steps to maximise the effectiveness of your preparation time:

*   Identify all the stakeholders and their motivations; Many will have different reasons why! Find out what these are or at worst have a good guess and proceed carefully until you have verified the guesses;
*   Ensure you have a strong reason why you want to achieve this outcome through the negotiations. This may be a personal reason, or an organisational reason;

strong reason why

121

clearly defined goal

check self-belief

possible resources

- Ensure that any key stakeholders either share this reason why, or have their own strong reason why. In this sense, key stakeholders are any people that you have to have on your side;
- Ensure that you have a clearly articulated, written goal, which is understood consistently by the negotiating team and any other key stakeholders. If you go into a negotiation without a clear goal, this will be reflected in your outcome – you cannot achieve a desired end result if there is any confusion about what that end result is. Equally, if you think you've done a great job in achieving the end result, but this isn't the end result that other stakeholders had in mind, this will cause you problems;
- Check your own self-belief, and that of the people in your team, to ensure that everyone believes the goal can be achieved. Use this opportunity to also test the strength of their reason why. If anyone is falling short in either of these areas, work to improve it. Ultimately, do not take anyone into a negotiation on your side of the table who does not have a strong reason why, or who does not understand the goal you are working to achieve, or who does not believe it is achievable. Otherwise, they will show this in their body language and this will weaken your position – good negotiators across the table will read doubts on the face of your team like a book;
- Know your facts. Have all the information you believe you could possibly need, and have it at your fingertips. Remember that a negotiating meeting isn't a memory test – as long as you know you have all the information you need with you, then that's fine. This can be in the heads of other people, or in notes, or on computer – the important thing is that you know what you might need and you know how to access it quickly. Use techniques such as mind maps or even a simple list. If you are not good with figures have a

ready reckoner worked out. Arrive at this point through possibility thinking – ask yourself what information could possibly be available to you which might help you to achieve your desired outcome. Think of all the people you could involve who can help you to define what information you may possibly need, or who may be able to provide it, and talk to them;

"Intelligence is not the ability to store information, but to know where to find it."
Albert Einstein

- Know the people in the room – yours, and theirs. If you are meeting people for the first time, see what you can find out from other people who may have dealt with them, but always keep an open mind. Sometimes people do not live up – or down – to their reputations. The important thing is how you build your own relationships. There is a maxim that says, "Build your relationships as soon as you can, because when you really need them you won't have time". This is not always possible, but make it possible wherever you can. Time spent on getting to know people you are going to negotiate with, whichever team they sit on, is never, ever, wasted;
- Do your homework so that you know who the key decision takers are on the other team. Are they in the room, or not? If the other team say they need to refer back to someone outside the negotiation, this may be tactical – and if you know the responsibilities of the people across the table you will be able to work this out, and use it to advantage;
- Work out how you are going to play the negotiations – who is leading the negotiation, and what roles others are going to play: who is going to present key facts and arguments, who is going to respond to various issues that will arise, how you are going to

involve others

123

signal any need for an adjournment. However, don't be too rigid – be prepared to think on your feet, and to adapt to the situation as the negotiation proceeds;

possibility thinking

- Develop your thinking around your opening and closing position, remembering to clearly articulate to your team what you are prepared to negotiate on, and what you are not. Carry out a further, detailed possibility thinking exercise around what you might do in any given situation. Engage your team through asking High Quality Questions – "If they do this, what will we do. And if they then respond in such and such a way, what will we do?" The more thinking you do ahead of the negotiation itself, around what might happen, the better prepared you will be. Preparation leads to confidence. Confidence breeds self-belief. Self-belief leads to better results;

parallel thinking

- Finally, consider all the tips above from THEIR point of view. Refer back to chapters 25-32 on Parallel Thinking. Assume that they are every bit as professional as you, and are spending time thinking through all their options, and finding out about your team in the same way that you are finding out about theirs. Use the following checklist:

1. Consider their reason (or reasons) why.
2. What possibilities are they thinking about?
3. Where might their opening and closing positions be?
4. What might they possibly offer to you that might have more value to you than to them, and is therefore relatively easily given?
5. How strong is their self belief?
6. What roles are they likely to play?
7. Who is leading their team? – this isn't always as obvious as you might wish it to be.

55. How do you start the negotiating meeting in a way that sets the right mood?

There are certain essentials that you can easily put in place to ensure that a negotiation gets off to the best possible start. These are useful in setting the tone even for a negotiation which you expect to be difficult:

*   Get all the meeting logistics right – ensure everyone knows where they are going, when they need to be there, and when you expect the meeting to end. This helps people to make their travel plans at each end of the meeting;
*   Publish an agenda, and ideally agree the agenda with the other party before publication. This ensures that you are all starting from a shared understanding of what the meeting is about, and what is under discussion. Be prepared to be flexible as the meeting progresses – agendas are for guidance and should not be viewed as rigid;
*   Order refreshments for the start of the meeting, and throughout the day as appropriate;
*   Ensure that you offer to explain where the facilities such as toilets and break-out areas or rooms are, on arrival;
*   Introduce yourselves, and give opportunity for others to introduce themselves, before the meeting formally starts. People like to be recognised as people. Avoid social gaffs like introducing yourself as if for the first time to someone you have actually met before;
*   At the beginning of the meeting, run through the agenda and ask if that's okay;
*   Make whatever opening remarks are appropriate and invite the other party to do the same.

Courtesy never portrays weakness.

125

56. How do you assess the confidence and authority of the other party?

Confidence, and authority, are different things. Someone can be very confident without having authority, and vice versa.

Confidence is easiest to recognise. If you think of your own team, and how you feel, then you will know that if you have prepared well, and have developed your Self-Belief, then you can't really avoid walking into the negotiating meeting with an air of confidence. This is exactly what you want to achieve – a sense in the room that you are there to do business, you expect to achieve, and you are prepared for the discussions that lie ahead no matter what comes up.

"Belief in a thing makes it happen."
Frank Lloyd Wright

Just as people can see this in you, so too can you see it in others. Confident people will engage in eye contact, will appear relatively calm and relaxed, and will appear in control both of themselves and of their team; issues that come up in the discussions will not fluster them. People who become loud or aggressive are generally trying to hide something – a lack of confidence in their own ability, or a lack of flexibility in the negotiating mandate they are working to.

Authority, on the other hand, can be more difficult to assess. The person who appears to have all the authority in a discussion may only be carrying out the bidding of someone else – and that person may, or may not, be in the room. There are signs to look for when assessing authority:

- What can you find out about the other team before the negotiations commence? Talk to people who know them, or have worked with them before. Involve people within your organisation who may know the answer, or people outside, perhaps through industry networking groups;

- Check with the other side who will be leading for their team before the negotiations commence. Look on the internet to see if there are reports of agreements reached by that individual, often in company press releases;

- Who across the table uses the term 'I' rather than 'we'?

- Watch the body language of team members when each is speaking. If the whole team pays great attention to things said by a particular person then chances are they have some position of authority within the talks;

- Does the other team have to adjourn at key points? If so, are they checking back with someone not in the negotiation?

- Are the talks getting bogged down, and then restarting with greater progress a few days later? This may indicate that people across the table are reticent to take decisions without referring back to an individual, Board or committee.

involve others

Very occasionally, it will occur in negotiations that the other team have not brought a decision taker with them. In such circumstances, it can become difficult to make progress. It may be necessary to suggest to the other side, perhaps informally, that it would be helpful if decisions could be made during the meeting, and that they may wish to consider involving key players directly in the talks. Be as diplomatic as possible – denting someone's ego is easily done and rarely brings you any benefits.

127

57. What choice of tactics do you have other than playing hardball or being cooperative?

It is helpful to think of tactics in terms of a comprehensive toolbox, from which you can draw the right piece of equipment to carry out each part of a task. Great negotiators will chop and change to meet changing needs. So, you need to be aware of what tactics work for you best in any given situation, and to be prepared to change tactics mid-flow to achieve your goals. We'll look at how you might do this in a few moments.

Whether you are going to play hardball, or be more cooperative, mainly depends on whether your negotiation is a one-off, or whether it is part of an actual, or possible, long-term relationship. If a one-off, and you roll someone over in a negotiation, achieving a win for you but a lose for them, then they'll remember that for ever. If you then find it wasn't a one-off, be prepared, because human nature will make them do everything possible to do to you what you did to them. This doesn't mean you won't be able to form long-term profitable relationships, but it does make it harder.

Be likeable!

Let's look at buying a house. You want to get the house as cheaply as possible, and the seller wants to get as much as they can. If you go in really hard, and don't seek to build any particular relationship with the sellers, don't expect all the holes to be filled, or the house to be clean when you move in, or indeed everything you expected to be there to be there (regardless of the legal niceties). If you can't work the boiler, don't expect any help if you ring the seller to ask their advice. Spending a little time to forge a relationship might not guarantee a better result, but it will help, because people like to deal with people they like.

Whatever kind of negotiation you are in, there are different stages which require potentially different approaches. You will have considered these possibilities as part of your preparation. Typically, in the early stages of a negotiation, there will be an element of position taking, and information sharing. In the house buying situation, the seller will be emphasising the features and benefits of their house – all the work they have done to improve it, how house prices are going up in the area, proximity to (or indeed distance from) local schools, depending on what they know about your situation. Not everyone wants a school behind their back garden, but some do…

This information sharing phase applies equally to commercial negotiations. Each party is seeking to influence the thinking of the other, to set expectations, and to appear constructive through providing information that might be of assistance to their desired outcome. Each party may well be using questioning as a technique to seek out information that is relevant to them, and to test what the other side is saying – looking for inconsistencies in information given, and seeking to understand whether what they are hearing fits with their own understanding of the situation.

In a truly collaborative negotiation, where each party recognises that they are part of a profitable, mutually beneficial relationship, there is often a significant degree of effort being put in by each side to help the other: "Would it help your position if I was to say that we could take delivery in four weeks instead of two?" Or, "What if we guaranteed your company first option on the new version of our product?" Skilled negotiators will recognise this tactic, which is as much to do with strengthening the relationship as it is to do with closing the deal – but closing the deal is always the purpose of the relationship, and this should never be forgotten.

**"To stay ahead, you must have your next idea
waiting in the wings."
Rosabeth Moss Kanter**

As the bargaining stage of the negotiation is entered, tactics might need to change. This reflects the fact that negotiations are often, by their nature, combative. We know that each party is seeking to maximise the benefit to themselves – perhaps less aggressively in an established and long-term relationship, but that depends on the nature of the relationship between the key players, as well as the personalities involved. There are some big egos in the world of negotiations.

So, during the heart of the negotiation, playing hardball may be more appropriate; use of phrases such as, "That won't work for us," or even that most liberating of all negotiating phrases, "no," might increase. Ultimately, however, it takes both sides to make an agreement and therefore unless one party is in an absolutely invincible position, and the other party has an absolute need to close a deal regardless of the terms of that deal (which happens, but is rare), then an agreement must be reached. And for an agreement to be reached, both parties need to believe that they are getting some benefit from the deal, even if it is unequal in value terms.

There are a number of ways to change tactics during a negotiation. Consider using the following checklist:

1. Summarise where you are up to in the conversation, to slow the mood down, and perhaps go back to an earlier point in the negotiation. There is nothing that says you can't write off a whole period of discussion if you don't like where it's got to, and go back;

2. Take an adjournment. This is a particularly helpful way of calming down a discussion that has become heated, which is all too easy when there is a lot at stake for each party;

3. Tell an engaging story. This can be related to something said, whether relevant or not. The point is that you can change the mood of a meeting by effectively taking 'time out' during the conversation itself – an adjournment without leaving the room. As a tactical manoeuvre, used sparingly but well, you can take the negotiation in a completely different direction when the discussions proper resume, perhaps even subtly changing the subject away from some area you don't particularly want to discuss;

4. Question whether it is possible to reach a deal at all. If you have prepared well, you will know something about how strongly the other team want to reach an agreement. If you know they are strongly motivated to reach a deal, but the talks are getting bogged down, this can force more focus into the discussions. Be careful not to threaten to walk away from the negotiating table, however, unless you are prepared to do it. Empty threats reduce your credibility. Real threats are only made if you know you can afford to walk away, remembering that this may also damage your relationship with the other team – and in the long run this may cost you, so take it into account.

Possible ways to change tactics.

58. Can relationships between negotiators become so close that they become a problem?

That depends on the nature of the relationship, and the qualities of the individuals concerned. It is certainly the case that close relationships do form between professional negotiators who deal with each other on a regular basis. Knowing that this can be an issue is sufficient for most people to check from time to time that they are still getting the right value out of the relationship – involving others to peer review your results gained through recent negotiations can be useful.

Many companies have established rules about the giving and receiving of corporate hospitality, including gifts and other inducements that can be used to attract business or to influence the opinion of people prior to negotiations. As a general principle, whether you are giving or receiving hospitality in whatever form, if it is too lavish for the circumstances, it can become problematical. Bear in mind also that it is not just what it looks or feels like to you that is the issue here – it is the impression that may be made on others. If you give the impression that you can be bought, this will undermine your integrity in the eyes of other people, even if it isn't true. And if you use lavish gifts to curry favour in other people, and to influence how they feel towards you, your company, or your products or services, don't be surprised when someone else takes that client from under your nose with a bigger, better deal.

Consider the possible risks.

59. If you are negotiating as part of a team, what do you do to ensure the people on your team understand what their role is, and work together effectively?

The first thing to do is to assemble the right team to support you in the negotiations. There are several reasons why you might choose someone to be on your team:

* They are a skilled negotiator;
* They have specialist knowledge you may need;
* They have an established relationship with a key person on the other side;
* You need their buy-in or involvement from a political point of view;
* You want them there to develop their skills and abilities.

It is important that each team member knows why they are there, what you expect of them, and what their role is. The only way to achieve this is through open dialogue and, if appropriate, rehearsal – all as part of your preparation for the negotiation.

**"Choose well, your choice is brief,
and yet endless."
Johann Wolfgang Von Goethe**

Consider using the following questions:

1. What skills do you require on your negotiating team?
2. What information do you require at your fingertips, and who can provide it as part of your team?
3. Who do you know who has previous experience of the people you will be negotiating against, and could they contribute as part of your team?
4. When is the right time to pull your team together, and carry out detailed preparation prior to the negotiation?
5. Who have you worked with before who is effective in this kind of situation?
6. Who might you involve for 'political' reasons, perhaps because they are close to people who are important to you?
7. Will role-playing help as part of your preparations?
8. How will you define and explain the roles that you want members of the team to play?
9. How will you explain the rules of the negotiation, such as the circumstances in which your team can call an adjournment, and how this should be signalled to you?

Remember to take account of the chemistry between people. There is no room for point scoring amongst members of the team in a negotiation – this weakens your position, and the team as a whole, and cannot deliver you a better result. Equally, there is no room for ill-discipline in a team.

**"When you have decided what you believe,
what you feel must be done,
have the courage to stand alone
and be counted."
Eleanor Roosevelt**

If things look as if they might go wrong on your team, call an adjournment and sort it out. If you have to, be ruthless: I have been known to call an adjournment, and then go back into the room with one fewer person than I started with. Explain to the meeting that X has unexpectedly been called away. They'll suspect the truth, especially if they have seen any discord between you, but that is better than carrying on with a dysfunctional team. And it will reinforce your position in the eyes of your negotiating opponents, which will do you no harm.

Teams that work together, and get to know each other as people rather than just as colleagues, work better together. Always show interest in your people, and in what is important to them. This is time well spent, and will increase the satisfaction and enjoyment of your people, who will feel more valued and cared for.

Finally, always celebrate your successes with your team. It's their success as well.

60. How do you go about establishing what your goal is before a negotiation starts?

A goal should be written, and ideally SMART:

*   Specific
*   Measurable
*   Achievable
*   Relevant
*   Timebound

See chapter 15 for more detail on defining goals.

Defining, and agreeing, a goal is often a negotiation in itself. As a negotiator, you need to ensure that you can agree a goal which you have a strong Reason Why to implement, which you believe you can deliver, and which has buy-in from all the people who can have an impact on the success of the negotiation.

Goal defining is easiest when it is very clear that something needs to be achieved, and where the solution is obvious. However, the most obvious solution is not always the best. So, in goal defining, as with every other aspect of the negotiation, carry out a possibility thinking exercise to look at all of the various ways in which you might achieve a solution. Once you have identified the most appropriate solution – ideally involving your own team in order to get their buy-in – sell your ideas to those who have authority, and whose support you need.

61. How do you get buy-in to that goal from the key people in your own organisation?

The best way to sell your ideas is to identify a strong Reason Why, which is appealing to those people who you need to support you. Consider their motivations, and appeal to their self-interest. If there is something in it for them, they will give you support.

Generally, there will be a sensible reason why a negotiation is necessary and appropriate – something needs to be achieved which is beneficial to your side. Set this out as a clear negotiating goal, in the SMART way that we have set out earlier. This should adequately describe what it is you intend to do, by when, and against what measures of success. The clearer and more appealing the goal, the easier it is to sell.

Accomplished negotiators will often say that they have greater difficulty in selling ideas to their own side than they do once they get into the negotiations themselves! When you analyse why this is, it becomes clear: if, as a negotiator, you have thought of something which you want to achieve, then the first time your own side hear your thoughts, they are coming at it cold. However, once you have got the negotiations themselves underway, the other team have already thought about it and have seen that there may be some advantage to themselves – otherwise they wouldn't be there.

Possibility thinking
- ways to communicate
my goals to others
- ways to gain buy-in.

Therefore, treat the selling of an idea to your own side as a negotiation in its own right, because that is exactly what it is. Prepare fully, and execute brilliantly. You should have an advantage – you are in the best possible position to know what it is that will appeal to your own people, because you know them and what is important to them.

If, after following all the guidance in this book, you cannot achieve support for your desired goal, there is little point in expending effort to achieve it. Change the goal.

62. What should you consider when deciding on a venue – your place or theirs?

Much is written about venue; some negotiators argue that you should only negotiate on your premises, or on neutral territory. This suggests that you are at some disadvantage if you go into someone else's castle to progress your agenda.

Personally, I challenge the overuse of military imagery when talking about negotiations. Whilst there is almost always a sense of rivalry and competition in negotiations (and by no means is that limited to your team!), negotiating is ultimately a subtle art involving collaboration. Very, very rarely does a single party to the negotiations hold all the power and all the influence.

So, if we are going into a negotiation to collaborate in reaching an agreed outcome, we don't need to think in terms of military analogies – we aren't going to storm a castle!

"All of the significant battles are waged within the self."
Sheldon Kopp

The answer to the venue question is easy: if it's important to you, then it's important. If, on the other hand, it doesn't matter to you at all, then it doesn't matter. Where you do your negotiations has implications in your own head if you let it.

My preferred approach to venue selection is to consider where is most convenient logistically for most people, bearing in mind that members of your own team, and the other team, will undoubtedly have other responsibilities elsewhere, both before and after your meeting. It is always worth making a few sacrifices to make life easier for other people, within reason. This kind of positive behaviour will help build relationships, will convey to the other party that you are flexible and helpful, but will not make you look like a soft touch. Once the negotiation itself starts, people will soon see what you are made of, and what you stand for.

I have negotiated alone, against a large team, on their premises, and have achieved great deals. Once, I wandered into the meeting and, with a smile, wryly observed, "There are 11 of you, and one of me, but I don't want you to feel inadequate in any way!" We then went on to do the deal, because I was confident of my own ability. Much earlier in my career I would not have been so comfortable in such a situation – so if this applies to you, don't put yourself there. You have a choice.

Thinking during the negotiation

As we move into the negotiation itself, we enter the most delicate phase. Some would argue that this is the hardest part. Preparing for a negotiation is one thing – and we have already seen all the things you can prepare for in order to maximise the likelihood of your success. However, once into the negotiation, anything can happen – and it usually does! An ability to think clearly under pressure, to be able to recall, when needed, all those elements that you covered in your preparations, and to be able to maintain a professional and calm approach even when things look as if they are moving against you, are vital.

A helpful self-talk statement.

Remember the saying, "There is nothing that cannot be turned to advantage". As long as you believe this essential truth, you will be fine – your Self-Belief cannot fail you if you accept the sense of this saying. Because even if someone throws something completely unexpected at you in the negotiation, there is always, always, a way to turn that to your advantage. The issue then becomes simply one of finding it!

63. How do you think on your feet?

We all admire people who are there with a ready answer, in the heat of the discussion. Nothing ever seems to surprise them, catch them off guard, or weaken them.

Negotiators who look as if they are thinking on their feet are generally those who have prepared well, and who use that preparation in the heat of discussion to best effect. They are actually recalling earlier, detailed work, rather than making it up as they go along. Just as a highly trained athlete makes the race look effortless, so too the experienced negotiator will have trained to overcome whatever obstacles and situations they may face.

By considering as many of the issues that may come up, and what you and your team will do in every set of circumstances you can think of, you will not only be able to think on your feet, but you will also build your self-confidence levels. This is a virtuous circle — the more prepared you are, the more confident you become, and the better able to achieve your goals.

In every negotiation, issues will arise that cause you and your team to need to think as the negotiation proceeds. An understanding of the ten possibility thinking areas will enable you to carry out a rapid, but effective, possibility thinking exercise, providing you with options as to how to respond. If you need more than a few moments of thinking time, either agree with the other team that you will park an issue, and take a note to come back to it later, or take an adjournment and work the issue with your team. Brainstorm those areas which apply to the difficulty you are facing, remembering that the solution might not lie in the most obvious place:

See chapter 37 for more about how to 'flood' the mind with HQQs.

- What possible tasks or things could help you in achieving your goal?
- What possible resources might be useful?
- What possible reasons are there to involve others? How might they help you?
- Who could possibly help you?
- How could you communicate your goal to them?
- How could you possibly obtain their help and get them committed to helping you?
- What possible obstacles might you encounter?
- What possible risks or implications might there be in pursuing your goal?
- How could you possibly overcome those obstacles and minimise any risks?
- What assumptions might you be making? What might you be taking for granted?

Ten possibility thinking areas to explore.

64. What tactics are available for setting the mood at the start of a potentially difficult meeting?

A positive mood at the start of a meeting is never going to get in the way of achieving a successful outcome. It doesn't matter how difficult the issue, or how strongly emotions are running. Imagine the worst kind of negotiation you can go into. Possibly it is to tell a supplier that you need to renegotiate your arrangements with them, reduce the size of your regular order, and reduce the price you pay for each unit you will be taking. You know that they rely on your business, and that this will have a deep impact on them. Or it might be a negotiation with a union at which you are looking to close part of your operation, resulting in compulsory job losses amongst a valued workforce. The kind of meeting where you know you've got to do it, but you don't want to.

So, how do you set the mood appropriately?

First, the logistics are important – the obvious things that can cause great irritation if they are not right:

- Does everyone know what the meeting is about, where it is, when it starts, and how long it is intended to go on? This ensures people can make appropriate diary and travel arrangements to enable them to concentrate on the matter in hand.
- Is the room big enough for the people who will be there?
- Have you arranged parking spaces for those who are travelling, and have reception been informed?
- Who will meet your guests if the meeting is on your premises?
- Have you arranged for refreshments on arrival, and any meals that might be appropriate? Remember that if a meeting is due to start say at 1pm, people who have travelled may not have had the opportunity for lunch, so having sandwiches available is a human touch.

"The future belongs to those who prepare for it."
Ralph Waldo Emerson

Second, ensure everyone knows each other before the meeting starts – do whatever introductions are appropriate. This can so easily be overlooked, especially if your mind is on the meeting itself. However negotiations are a people business and everyone wants to know who they are dealing with by name, and possibly a little background.

Third, if an agenda has been issued, ask if anyone wants to add anything to it. If no agenda has been issued, introduce the matters you wish to discuss and invite attendees to make any preliminary points.

If the meeting is about particularly difficult issues, say so. If you are about to discuss the kind of scenario we have outlined above, it is often appropriate to introduce the discussions by saying this is a difficult issue for all the participants; showing you are sensitive to peoples' feelings is a mark of your personal integrity, and what it is you stand for.

65. How can you say a proposal is no good without giving offence?

Firstly, bear in mind that in negotiations, people are expecting you to reject the terms of their proposals, particularly in the early stages. Very, very few negotiators will open with their final position – why would they – they might get a better deal than that through the negotiating process. After all, that's what it's all about – trying to get the best result for your side. So, it's difficult to cause offence when rejecting a proposal that they expect you to reject. They might well pretend to be shocked and horrified that you haven't appreciated just how fantastic their proposal is, and if you are facing a good negotiator that will look really genuine. But it isn't!

As negotiations progress, one of the best ways to say to someone that their proposal or position isn't working for you is to offer help: "I want to help you get this proposal to work for all of us, but it's just not there yet. Have you considered...?" What you really mean is that their position needs to change in order for you to accept it.

This can also be achieved using the word 'invite'. This is a great negotiating word:

• "May I invite you to reconsider your proposal in respect of the price and your suggested delivery date?"

- "I invite you to imagine how powerful it would be for both our companies if we were able to get to a deal – however these terms need further work." What you are doing is seeking to engage their imagination by focusing them on an image of success, whilst signalling that things have to be done by them to get there.

"He who has learned to disagree without being disagreeable has discovered the most valuable secret of a diplomat."
Robert Estabrook

The words you use are important – they give an impression of you, and they illustrate how you think, and what you are thinking about. If you have a generally collaborative style, where you are spending time and effort to understand the issues from their point of view as well as your own, application of the Go MAD Thinking approach will assist you to appreciate the best way to encourage progress from the other side.

It is always worth remembering, however, that the blunt approach can often reap dividends – a simple, "That's no good for us," or even, "No," is clear, unambiguous, and sets the scene for a response. As long as disagreements aren't allowed to become personal, it's more difficult to cause offence than you might imagine!

66. How do you assess the confidence and authority of the other party?

There are three ways in which people can give away how they are feeling:

- What they say;
- How they say it;
- Body language.

Learn to study each of these. Listen carefully, and watch how people look and sound.

If someone on the other team says something, and others on the team look down, or begin to lean away from the speaker, it indicates disagreement with what is said.

If someone is lacking in confidence, they may speak extremely quietly, or, conversely, loudly – possibly even aggressively – to try to cover up how they really feel.

If you hear someone say something you don't think they believe in, ask a question such as, "You can't possibly believe that?" and watch for their response.

"You've got to take the initiative and play your game. In a decisive set, confidence is the difference."
Chris Evert Lloyd

People may lack confidence because they don't believe in what they are saying, or because they don't believe they can deliver what is on offer. Again, probing with questions will elicit more information. If people do not have the authority to deliver, this will come out in the discussion through reference to a need to 'consider this carefully after the meeting' or to 'take soundings' or 'refer back'. This is not necessarily a problem – if something unexpected has come up in a discussion, which isn't covered in their negotiating mandate, it is quite normal to refer matters back to those who do have the authority. It only becomes a problem if it gets repeated frequently: then you need to consider whether you are negotiating with the right people.

67. How do you keep your eye on your goal as the negotiations progress?

Remember that old bit of advice at school that, in an exam, you should keep reading the question? We all know and admire our own creative ability to fire off in the wrong direction simply because that looks easier and more attractive! So, write down your negotiating goal, typically in a negotiating mandate, and refer to it often.

It is often easier than you might think to get the other team to depart from their own negotiating mandate – particularly if you are putting something in front of them that they weren't there to achieve, but which is inherently attractive to them. Don't let someone do the same to you. The dangers of either side going too far off track is that even if you reach an agreement, one or the other of you will not be able to deliver because people outside the negotiation in positions of authority will unpick what has been done.

Focus on the goal.

Be aware of the actions of your own team. If someone is going off-track, take an adjournment and sort it out. If the other team are going off-track, bring them back to the point. If necessary, take a little time out and address the issue informally.

The key is to recognise what you are there to do, and to stick to it. This doesn't mean being inflexible – if progress is possible on things that aren't your central focus of attention, or are peripheral to the deal, then progress them if they are valuable to you. Do this in addition to the deal you are aiming for, not in place of it.

68. How do you steer to a positive outcome?

Taking a positive mindset into the negotiation in the first place is where you start. This flows from:

- Knowing your subject;
- Having a clear goal;
- Preparing yourself and your team;
- Having the information you need at your fingertips;
- Researching the people you will be meeting;
- Carrying out a possibility thinking exercise, and rehearsing in your own mind, and with your team, how you will address all those issues you believe will come up.

Let your strong sense of self-belief walk into the room with you. Your own team, and the people you are negotiating with, will see this, and it will influence them towards a positive outcome.

In the meeting itself, use the resources at your disposal, and the tools and techniques which we have explored in this book, to drive the discussion towards a positive outcome.

Keep thinking possibilities.

If the conversation is not going in the direction you want – and this happens frequently at some stage of most negotiations – change course. Achieve this by changing tactics, or by taking a break and then summarising, when you regroup, from the point you would prefer to be at in the meeting. Take people away from the direction they are heading in by telling an engaging story – it doesn't have to be relevant to the negotiation in any way – it just needs to be interesting enough to break the mood or to take people's thinking in another direction.

If you are stuck, carry out an individual or team possibility thinking exercise to broaden your options. This can be done in the meeting, but is often best carried out in an adjournment. Use that adjournment to refocus your team on the goal.

69. How do you prevent being content seduced?

It is important to have all of the information you might need at every stage of the negotiation at your fingertips, whether this is in your head, on paper, on computer, in the heads of the rest of your team, or available from people outside the meeting. Gather this information as you prepare for the negotiation. It has two purposes; firstly, to assist you in dealing with any matters that might arise in the meeting. Second, to help you and your team with your Self-Belief.

It is equally important to bear in mind that you are highly unlikely to need all that information in the discussions. Indeed, many negotiations – especially those that focus on matters of principle rather than detail – can progress to a successful conclusion without any real detail at all. The key point is that you should use the information and detail you need – no more, and no less. No more because if you put detail on the table that is unnecessary, it may divert the discussions away from the key areas, and indeed may give the other party information to use against you. No less because you need to table everything that is relevant. Getting the balance right is a matter of judgement as the talks progress, however bear in mind that a negotiation is not a test of your ability to amaze the other side with how much you know.

**"The best informed man is not necessarily the wisest."
Dietrich Bonhoeffer**

As a general rule of thumb, when judging whether to put information forward, or whether to hold it back, ask yourself whether you think the information will move the discussion forward, or not. If you are not sure, keep it to yourself; you can always reveal it later if you need to.

147

70. What is the purpose of adjournments, and how can you call one without looking weak?

Adjournments are one of the most useful techniques in a negotiation. They can have a number of purposes:

- To give you and your team time to consider things said or done by either party, i.e. to give yourselves thinking time;
- To refocus yourself and your team on your goal and to ensure that you are driving the discussion in the right direction;
- To enable you to carry out a possibility thinking exercise if you want to give yourself more options;
- To change the mood of a meeting. If things are getting hot, an adjournment gives time for everyone to calm down;
- To enable you to contact people to give your views, opinions or information;
- To take a break. Intense negotiations can be very draining. Taking a 10-minute time out is good for you;
- To give you opportunity for informal or 'corridor' discussions with the other team;
- To take a natural break;
- To be seen to consider a point carefully, even if you know you can't give in on it. This is a tactical consideration which will be influenced by matters such as the mood of the meeting, and how well you know the other negotiators — if you think it appropriate to decline a proposition without an adjournment, do so.

Adjournments can be called by either side, at any point, and you do not need to give a reason. Simply announce that you wish to take an adjournment. Give the other team an idea of how long you plan to be, simply as a matter of courtesy, and if you think you will need more time, let them know. Some adjournments, particularly to consider complex matters, can take place over many hours, overnight, or even longer.

Agree amongst your team how adjournments will be flagged; typically this will be done by the lead negotiator, and it is always good practice to advise your team that you will call an adjournment if anyone wants one – ask your people to write you a note if they are not sitting next to you. One of your team might have spotted something that you haven't – and it might be important, so it's always worth taking a few moments out in such circumstances.

involve others

Do remember that many negotiations don't need any adjournments at all – they are a tool to use if they are useful, otherwise there's no point. A useful guiding principle is – if in doubt, adjourn.

71. How do you handle difficult situations that can occur during negotiations?

There are four types of difficult situation that are likely to occur during negotiations:

1. The other team throw something into the discussion that you are unprepared to deal with;
2. Someone, or some people, on the other team are simply not moving their position, and the negotiation is becoming bogged down, with no progress being made;
3. Emotions are getting out of hand and the temperature in the room is so high that progress is proving difficult;
4. Someone on your own team has gone off at a tangent and they are risking damaging your negotiating position.

possible obstacles

Let's look at each in turn:

The other team throw something into the discussion that you are unprepared to deal with.

No matter how well you carry out your preparation, there is always potential for something to be thrown into a negotiation that you are not prepared for. Let's say you are negotiating with a supplier around the arrangements for a conference venue. You have talked about the price and layout of the main rooms you will need, equipment hire, and accommodation for those who will stay overnight. You are happy with the catering arrangements. The only sticking point is overall price, and you want a reduction.

Instead of moving on price, the other negotiator offers a series of weekend breaks at other hotels within their group. You know that this is relatively inexpensive for them to give to you, especially if their hotels are not full to capacity at the weekends.

Your goal, however, is to achieve a deal at a certain price, and you need a reduction. You haven't prepared for this eventuality. What do you do?

A quick possibility thinking exercise either in your own head, or together with your team, will come up with ideas. Call an adjournment if needed, so you can consider these possibilities in private.

The first and most obvious point is that the other team are still willing to negotiate – so by throwing something else into the deal, they are trying to influence your thinking, just as you are trying to influence theirs. They are offering something that they feel may be of particular interest to you. So, is it? Do you send your successful sales people on weekend breaks with their family as a thank you for a job well done – in which case, this offer is worth more in value terms to you than it is costing them to give it. Or, would the weekend breaks be a useful prize to give away in an employee competition? Or do you hold any weekend conferences – you could suggest that this offer is packaged differently and that you hold a weekend conference in one location, which might save your organisation considerable expenditure which would otherwise have been incurred anyway. Or, you could ask them to double the number of weekend breaks to make it attractive to you – remembering that it won't necessarily cost them a significant amount of additional money to do so.

And if the weekend breaks do not have value for you in your particular circumstances, use this offer as a visible sign that they are prepared to continue negotiating. They haven't yet reached their bottom line, and more can therefore be shaved off the price.

Always keep your eye on your goal when something new is thrown into the debate, as it's so easy to be sidetracked by something that looks attractive, but which isn't what you are there to achieve.

Someone, or some people, on the other team are simply not moving their position, and the negotiation is becoming bogged down, with no progress being made.

Consider what tactics you might adopt to move the discussion forward again. Perhaps some time out is needed, to enable both sets of negotiators to refocus on their respective goals, or to give opportunity for people to take a break, or to carry out a possibility thinking exercise on what you might do next, or to change the mood of the meeting. Maybe you can use some time to obtain some further facts and information which might strengthen the power of your argument.

more possibility thinking

Consider whether you should 'park' the issue under discussion, which is proving at the moment to be a blockage. This means agreeing to come back to it later. And make a note of it, so you do come back to it – they may be hoping you forget. Often issues that bog down a negotiation at a particular point in time are easier to deal with at another point, when progress has been made on other issues. Sometimes something that is really important to one or the other teams becomes less important later.

If you can't park it, consider why it is such a blockage in the first place. Is this genuinely one of the other team's non-negotiables, that is, something on which they simply cannot budge? Or, is it negotiable, but they need further authority before they can do so – in which case, give them the opportunity to get that authority. This might mean adjourning the meeting and reconvening at a later date; or they may just need to make a phone call.

Think about whether they are adopting this approach for tactical reasons: they may be holding out for a concession from you on something that is of value to them, and they are just making you work for it. This tactic can be turned around by working out what is of most value to them, and offering to bargain – but ensure that the bargain is on your terms, not theirs.

Is the lack of movement on their side due to the fact that they have inexperienced negotiators? If this is the case, you may need to elevate matters, and to create the need for them to bring different people into the discussion, who may be more prepared to move.

Appreciate that they may have hit their bottom line – the point below which it is not worth their while to reach an agreement with you. Consider how you might indicate a preparedness to change your position if it will help them

Use HQQs to present "what if..." scenarios.

to move theirs. Use High Quality Questions to obtain a response without committing yourself to any particular course of action – "What if I was to offer xyz. Would this enable us to take the discussion forward?"

If all else fails, think about whether it is appropriate to take a considered risk – and you should always focus on the risks and implications of so doing: a question such as, "If we can't move this discussion forward, are we saying that these talks have effectively broken down?" will certainly grab the attention of the other side. But be prepared for what you will say and do if they say yes. You may have to make a major concession to restart the talks; or you may have to go home without a deal. It is always worth considering, at this point, who you think needs the deal more. If you need it more than them, don't take the risk.

Consider possible risks and implications.

Emotions are getting out of hand and the temperature in the room is so high that progress is proving difficult.

Ask yourself why the temperature is getting out of hand? Is it on your side of the table, or theirs, or both? Is it genuine annoyance, or is it tactical – emotions can be used powerfully to influence the thinking of others, particularly where one side of a negotiation senses that the other side doesn't like confrontation.

If it's genuine irritation, then there will be a reason for that. Either something said, or the way it has been said, has sparked anger – in which case it might be necessary to backtrack, or even to apologise; or perhaps someone is feeling under immense pressure, and this is coming cross as anger. Pressure can arise for a number of reasons, not least when someone feels they are being backed into a corner, and perhaps have given more ground than they wanted to.

"You cannot shake hands with a clenched fist."
Indira Gandhi

True anger, on any side of a negotiation, is an impediment to progress. People do not think clearly when they have lost their temper. Defuse the situation. Take a break. Allow things to cool down before recommencing the meeting with something positive, such as a summary of the things that have been agreed so far.

Someone on your own team has gone off at a tangent and they are risking damaging your negotiating position.

It's easy to get burned in the heat of the moment. In the middle of a negotiation, if one of your team is going away from the agreed track, you need to make a judgement as to whether this is going to assist you, or not. Even though you will have prepared carefully for the negotiation, you can never truly script the discussion, or accurately predict the order in which things will happen. Therefore, you need to be flexible – and if one of your team has come up with a brilliant argument that you did not prepare for, then let them get on with it if it is moving you towards your goal.

However, if this is not the case, and things look as if they may be going awry, then you need to bring the individual into line. Use whatever technique is most appropriate – pass them a note; or interrupt the flow and carry on the conversation in the direction you would prefer; or call an adjournment to refocus your team on the goal. Avoid, wherever possible, doing anything that looks to the other team as if you are chastising one of your own people in public. At best, it can be embarrassing, and at worst you'll make an enemy for life.

72. How can you identify when you should suspend negotiations and regroup?

The time to regroup is easy to recognise – it is whenever you feel things are not going to plan. This can be for a variety of reasons:

*   Something has occurred which, in spite of your detailed planning, you had not foreseen;
*   One of your team is going off at a non-productive tangent (and remember that not all tangents are necessarily bad – this is a judgement call you have to make);
*   The negotiation has become bogged down;
*   You need to break the mood of a negotiation – perhaps things are becoming a little heated;
*   You need to get the other team off a particular tack they are on, because it's not helping you;
*   You need to carry out some possibility thinking, or get some information from people either within your team, or outside it;
*   You need a break.

Just as you, as a good negotiator, will seek to help the other team to accept your proposals, so too will a good negotiator across the table from you. So if someone says, "Why don't we all take a break, it might do us some good," (and this can be said in a thousand different ways) ask yourself, "Are they trying to hint that I need to think about what they are saying some more?" or, "Do they want a corridor discussion?"

"The most important trip you may take in life is meeting people halfway." Henry Boyle

---

Equally, if you want to take the opportunity to float some

ideas with the leader of the other team without doing it in formal session, taking time out to do so, and then regrouping your thoughts and those of your team around a potential new position is a good idea.

73. How do you recognise when, and how, to change your position to best effect?

Virtually any negotiation will start with each team (and there may be more than two teams in a negotiation) setting out their respective positions. These are generally starting positions – no experienced negotiator opens with their closing position unless they absolutely hold all the power – and this is exceedingly rare. Thereafter, through discussion, each party will look for the overlap between their position, and the position of the other parties. The aim is always to settle as close to your own opening position as you can.

It follows that movements of position will therefore be influenced by the opinion of each team as to what is acceptable in the discussion – and therefore not all movements are identical, either within your own team, or between teams. For example, if you want to sell desk lamps at £20 a unit, and a potential buyer opens at £10 a unit, and then moves to £12, your next move does not have to be £2. It could be 50p, or less.

The key to knowing when to move position is recognising when you need to do so to move the negotiation forward.

When to move my negotiating position.

In the desk lamp example, imagine that you open at a selling price of £20, and the buyer says, "I can only pay £10". You could say, "£20 is a great price for this quality, delivery is immediate, and we're prepared to extend our normal 7 days credit time to 28 days". If the other negotiator then says, "Okay, we'll pay £12 on that basis," you could respond, "£12, no way, the price is £20 for those terms". The other team may then say, "Well we couldn't go over £14," and they've moved their position twice without you conceding much, especially if you always intended to give 28 day terms anyway. So maybe they'll move their position again. Maybe to their business, credit terms are more important than the price, because possibly they have cash flow issues. The point is, only move your position when it is clear that the discussion can go no further if you do not, and then move as little as you can get away with.

74. Traditional negotiating – i.e. where the parties take up positions, conceal their hand, send coded signals and trade concessions… – What are the benefits of taking this approach?

I would describe this kind of approach as common, rather than traditional, and the benefits are that this is the best way to get a deal.

Remember that the simplest definition of negotiating is 'influencing the thinking of others'. We have already seen that any negotiation is, in essence, collaboration between parties to reach agreement on something. It follows that each party will want something out of the negotiation, and it is a rarity indeed for all parties to want exactly the same thing. Therefore, each will have its desired best outcome, its bottom line, and between the two the area in which it is prepared to do a deal – but the nearer to the ideal position you can get, the better.

In virtually any negotiation each side will put forward arguments as to why their best position is the most desirable outcome for everyone, and indeed you will generally expect negotiators to start beyond their ideal position – because if, by some chance, they can overachieve against their own view of the best they can reasonably hope to do, then so much the better. In truth, however, each party to a negotiation knows that the other side is going to leave themselves some room for manoeuvre. As the discussions progress, there may indeed be coded signals – "That's not working for me, but what if I were to..." sends a signal without making a commitment. And each party will look for things that they can give which mean more to the other team than they do to them. Trading concessions in this way is all part of moving the debate forward towards a satisfactory outcome for all.

75. How do you deal with difficult people that won't move position?

The first thing to do is to seek to understand why the individual is being difficult, or is not moving:

- Is it merely a tactical ploy? If so, stick with your position – somebody has to move eventually, and it doesn't have to be you. You can always signal that you might be prepared to move, as long as there is movement on the other side as well – it doesn't commit you to actually move your position!
- Are you seeking to negotiate what, for them, is a non-negotiable? In which case, you can drop the point, if it isn't too important to you in the overall scale of things, or park it and come back to the point later;
- Things might look different for either, or both, sides, if agreement has been reached in other key aspects of the negotiation;
- Are they being difficult because they are under pressure? Not everyone who negotiates is either good at it, or indeed comfortable with it. Help the person to help you; take steps to build trust. Once they appreciate that you are not out to get them they may become less difficult;

HQQs to focus the mind.

- Are they simply a difficult person to get on with? Such people do exist. Look for the parts of the person's behaviour and personality that you do like, and work on that. Focus on other members of their team – can progress be made that way?
- Do they actually have negotiating authority? If not, suggest that they adjourn to take instructions. If progress is not possible, you need to reconvene the negotiations with someone on the other side who can make decisions;
- Consider, through parallel thinking, what is going through their mind. What is it that is causing them to be that way? Are they simply going through the motions, and actually they don't want a deal at all?

parallel thinking

The action you can take to move the discussion forward will depend on the answers to the above questions – but remember that there is ultimately only one situation in which a negotiation will become truly stuck, and that is where one or other of the parties is simply not prepared to reach agreement on the terms available. Therefore, something has to change.

It is also worth remembering at this point that someone who is being utterly unhelpful to you one day may be perfectly reasonable the next – you do not know all the pressures they are under, personally or professionally, even though you should always do your best to find out.

76. How do you influence hospital consultants and GPs who perceive themselves to be of a higher status than managers?

Ask yourself the question, "Why does this individual, or these people, perceive themselves to be of a higher status than me, and does it matter?"

A feeling of status might be just that – by virtue of individual perception, some people feel the need to convey their level of status – but if it isn't impeding your ability to achieve results through your negotiations, then ignore it.

Where, however, it is becoming a problem, you need to deal with it, and there are a number of effective remedies, some of which require quite a bit of patience and diplomacy – keeping your eye firmly on your goal, which is to influence their thinking and not to score a point or get on their nerves simply because they may be getting on yours!

- Acknowledge what they are good at, and what they bring to the discussion which you cannot – areas of expertise built up by many years of training and then practice. Then remind them of what you are good at, and what you bring to the discussion that they don't. You are seeking here to build mutual respect for each others' contribution, and to build a better appreciation of your status – but not in a way that could appear competitive;
- Spend time seeking to build a personal relationship – the initial problems may be that they simply do not know you, and therefore do not know your capabilities;
- Focus on some past successes, and share positive stories;
- Appeal to their sense of self-interest by explaining how what you want to do will make their lives easier in some way;
- Take care to listen to their concerns or issues and give them airtime without dismissing them out of hand.

"I like to listen. I have learned a great deal from listening carefully. Most people never listen."
Ernest Hemingway

The skills you have as a negotiator will play a full role in this situation. Arriving at a solution, for instance on agreeing a way forward, is as much a negotiation as any other. They may not see it this way, so subtlety and discretion is certainly in order, avoiding giving the impression that you are actually negotiating with them.

Ultimately, you have a job to do, just as they do, and people who are unreasonable in any way can't be allowed to prevent you from doing it. It's always a judgement question on what techniques will best work. If they are a key stakeholder with an interest in the outcome of the negotiation, but are not directly involved, invite them to join the team or even lead it. They'll probably run a mile and then you'll find yourself in a much improved situation!

77. How do you take the heat out of situations?

At the right time, bringing a little heat into a negotiation can be a good tactical ploy – perhaps to convey your strength of feeling on a particular matter, or to direct the attention of the other party away from somewhere you don't want them to go.

Recognising the value of this tactical ploy, consider the reason why the other party might introduce heat into the discussions. There is a difference between tactical heat, and genuine raw emotion. The former is just part of the discussion, and you simply need to carry on. The latter can become a problem because someone who is losing their temper (on whichever side) is losing their ability to think properly, and is therefore putting themselves at a negotiating disadvantage.

If the other party is getting hot under the collar, there are a number of ways to defuse the situation:

See chapter 37 about identifying hindering thinking components.

- Respond to points made in a calm, quiet and composed fashion – even if your own emotions are running high. The other party may begin to mirror your behaviour;
- Work to find out what is causing the heat. Are they feeling threatened, perhaps because they are moving too far from their agreed position, or because you're 'winning' the argument as they see it, or because they are beyond their level of competence as a negotiator? Consider adapting your tone and approach – if the discussion is going your way, you may be able to be a little less forceful;
- Call an adjournment – time out of the discussions gives everyone the opportunity to refresh, discuss issues with their team, refocus the discussions, or simply just rest;
- If you don't want to break up the discussion at that point for whatever reason, summarise where you are up to – focusing significantly on any areas of agreement, or on what is going best; keeping it positive can rub off on the other side;
- Acknowledge that things are getting a little fraught, and that everyone needs to keep things on an even keel. Simply acknowledging that you are aware of the situation is often enough to change the mood.

If things are getting bad tempered on your side of the table, use the same techniques, but direct them towards wherever the issue is. A comment such as, "We all feel strongly about this but let's keep things in check," might be all that is required. A mild rebuke, even in front of the other team, is only a problem for you if you (and your team) let it be. Otherwise, take an adjournment, or a comfort break, and deal with the situation in private.

78. How do you politely tell people to shut up?

The short answer is that it depends how well you know them, and what you can get away with!

However, think about the situation a little more broadly. An individual on the other team who goes on and on, perhaps repeating things that have already been said, or just generally using lots of words which aren't driving the discussion forward, might be helpful to you. If someone on the other team is boring their colleagues, that in itself might help to motivate them towards a solution. The key question is, "Could this situation help me, or is it hindering?"

**"I will go anywhere as long as it is forward."
David Livingstone**

If it's a problem, or is clearly using valuable time that you can't afford to lose, consider using one of the following phrases:

- "That's all well and good, but this isn't moving things forward. We need to focus on…"
- "I don't find that helpful. What I would find helpful would be…."
- "I hear what you are saying. I'd be interested to hear other views about…"
- "Thank you. Perhaps we'll come back to that. Can we now discuss…"

choices

If you know the person well, and you know you aren't likely to cause offence either to the individual or indeed to other people on their team (who may not of course know you quite so well) you can always be more bold: "You've certainly done that one to death!" or "I always enjoy it when you get onto your favourite subject!" There is always

163

room for appropriate humour and use of your personality in discussions, and chances are everyone in the room will thank you, even if they may not admit it out loud!

79. It would be difficult for even a skilled commercial negotiator to take on the management brief in employee relations negotiations. What are your thoughts on the fact that there is little carry-over between these two negotiating situations?

Negotiation skills are highly generic, and there is very little – if any – difference in the skill-set needed between a negotiator who does commercial deals such as buying and selling, and an employee relations negotiator.

There are, however, often differences both in the subject matter of the negotiations, and in some aspects of how they might be conducted.

Employee relations negotiations will typically be between representatives of an employer, and representatives of employees – probably elected from the workforce, perhaps as part of a staff association or a trade union. The subject matter is almost invariably about concepts, ideas and proposed actions rather than physical things – but the skills required to sell ideas as distinct from products or services is exactly the same.

Sometimes negotiations will be required by law, such as discussions on changes to terms and conditions which are governed by contract law, or discussions around business changes that may lead to job cuts which are governed by employment law. And sometimes they will be driven by agreements you already have, say to negotiate bonus schemes with a union even though they are discretionary arrangements rather than contractual.

Staff representative bodies will often invest as much time in training their key people in negotiation skills as any other negotiators. Interestingly, it is not unknown for employers to make an assumption that managers will be able to negotiate effectively against negotiators who are actually far more highly trained, and more experienced in negotiation, than they are. Any such imbalance is avoidable with a little forethought.

Another potential difference is that each team may comprise people who have to be there for political reasons rather than because of any particular expertise or contribution they may make. Be aware of who is sitting across the table from you, what their influence is inside and outside the room, and never write off someone who remains silent as irrelevant.

Other than that, the rules are exactly the same, the skills are as for any other negotiation, and the achievement of mutually agreed solutions to problems is just as satisfying.

80. What happens when you are, or feel, powerless in a negotiation?

Are you powerless, or do you just feel powerless? There is a difference, and it's really important to be able to distinguish one from the other.

Rarely is one party in a negotiation completely powerless – even if the extent of the power of one team over the other is more to do with perception than reality! However, if you are feeling powerless, use the Go MAD Thinking System to establish where those feelings come from. More often than not the issue will be to do with your level of Self-Belief, or the lack of clarity of your goal. By working with your team, and through involving other people who aren't party to the negotiation, you can work to clarify your goal, and to strengthen your self-belief.

Identify which of the four thinking components are most hindering.

165

Ask helpful possibility based HQQs.

Occasionally one side of a discussion really does hold all of the cards. If you are faced by this situation, ask yourself the following question: "What could I possibly do to give the other side the impression that I hold more power and influence in this discussion than I really do?" If you are not hugely confident, what can you do to convey the image that you are?

**"Confidence, like art,
never comes from having all the answers;
it comes from being open to all the questions."
Earl Gray Stevens**

If you send out signals through what you say, how you say it, and your body language, which lead the other party to believe that you are absolutely desperate for a deal, they will react accordingly. They will drive a tougher bargain, nearer to their ideal position or perhaps even beyond it, if they feel they can. Were the roles reversed, you would do the same, taking into account the need ultimately to preserve the integrity of your relationships if you need a longer-term arrangement with them. Therefore, giving an impression that you feel powerless will not help your situation.

If you truly are up against all the odds, then take whatever deal you can that is better than your walk away position and direct your energies to avoiding getting in that situation ever again. Think of it as a learning experience – always look for the positives in the situation, remembering that, in one way or another, there is nothing that cannot be turned to advantage.

81. What place does aggression have in negotiation?

We have seen that tactical annoyance in a discussion, to clearly convey in no uncertain terms your strength of feeling about a particular aspect of the negotiations, can be useful. The point is that it needs to be controlled, used sparingly, and for short durations. Otherwise, you either begin to lose credibility, or worse still you genuinely lose your temper. If you lose your temper, regardless of the provocation, you begin to lose your ability to think rationally, calmly and sensibly. Excess adrenalin prepares not only your body for the fight or flight reaction, but also your brain; in such circumstances your mind will close down unnecessary thinking functions and will concentrate solely on what is needed for fight or flight. This narrows your options considerably, and the only way to get back on an even keel is to calm down, perhaps by taking an adjournment.

It follows that there is no role in negotiations for true aggression. So, when an experienced negotiator becomes aggressive, they are most likely using it as a tactic. Ask yourself why. What are they trying to achieve? What are they trying to stop you talking about, or finding out? What was being said, perhaps by someone on their team, immediately prior to any outburst?

Think in questions.

If someone on the other team is genuinely aggressive, again, ask yourself why? Are they covering up inexperience, or discomfort of some kind? Why do they feel threatened? Do you need to help them to relax, so that they can function better – improved thinking leads to better deals all round, so don't let the situation fester.

167

82. What do you do when a negotiation starts to go wrong?

I think it's fair to say that during any negotiation there is always at least one point where something happens that you wished hadn't. This is because negotiations involve people, and people can be unpredictable. Therefore, they come to the table with their own views, opinions, goals, agendas, prejudices and needs.

Careful preparation, as we have seen, is the most effective way of planning what to do when things come up that you would prefer to steer clear from. However, as you cannot script a negotiation, because there is more than one party at the table, it is wise to have at your disposal a few techniques to help you deal with the unexpected:

- Do some possibility thinking – ask yourself the question, "What could I possibly do or say which might move this discussion in the direction I desire?" Or, "What information might I be able to obtain which could help me, and where can I get it?"
- Do something to change the course of the conversation. Tell an engaging story which might take people's attention away from somewhere it's headed that you don't want to go;
- Summarise the discussion so far, emphasising those areas that are of importance to you and see if you can then restart the conversation somewhere else;
- Take an adjournment. This gives you time to think about your next steps, and also helps to break the mood of the discussion;
- Say, "No". This can be a liberating word – as long as you don't overuse it, such a brief rejection of a position put forward from the other side can stop a conversation in its tracks;

- Use a tactical ploy, such as pretending to get annoyed
  – but don't get annoyed for real as you will reduce
  your own ability to think calmly, rationally and
  effectively – which is exactly what you need to be
  when you are under pressure.

Above all, remain focused on your goal. When things start
to go awry, there is often real pressure to compromise on
your goal. Resist the temptation, because that will lead you
down a path to a conclusion that you don't want, and are
not there to achieve.

**83. It's often very useful to take time in the middle
of a negotiation to think through options and
possibilities before you respond to a particular
point or situation. What techniques can you
use to buy thinking time during a pressurised
discussion?**

Buying time is easy. Nobody can stop you taking time out
to think – although they might try.

**"Thinking is the essence of wisdom."
Persian Proverb**

Imagine you are in the middle of a heated negotiation. The
other team think things are going well for them, and that
you have made more movement than they have.
Recognising that you need to regroup, you say, "We need
to take a brief adjournment to consider our position in
light of what you have said". In an effort to maintain
momentum, the other side say, "But we're nearly there.
This is a bad time to take an adjournment. Let's just focus
on…" or, "We need to be away at half past because we've
a plane to catch".

They might even sound reasonable.

169

Your answer should be, "We'll come right back to that when we return. I'll let you know if we intend to be out for more than 15 minutes". And if that's no good, adjourn the meeting to another day.

The point is, you only feel pressurised to do something you don't want to do if you let yourself be pressurised. You have ultimate control over what you let into your head. So, if you are being put under intense pressure by the other side, ask yourself why – why are they pushing so hard? What's in it for them? You can be assured that they think it's helping their situation, not yours – so don't play along.

84. How do you use the power of high quality questions to achieve your goal?

See chapters 34-36 about HQQs.

High Quality Questions – or HQQs – are such an important technique that several chapters of this book are dedicated to them. We often think in questions – questions we ask ourselves, questions we imagine other people asking of us, and questions we would like others to answer for us. Asking and answering HQQs is one of the best ways to engage your imagination, and that of your team.

The best HQQs are the ones that stimulate thinking and, if answered, will move the negotiation in the direction you want to go. They can be used to help you understand a complex point, or to check that someone on the other team has understood what you have said. They can be used to test out an idea without actually formally committing to it – as in, "What if I were to reduce the price to £x and guarantee delivery within three weeks?" You haven't said you are going to do it, but you are finding out what their response would be if you did.

There is a really powerful HQQ that you can ask of yourself and of your team in times of need – for instance when under pressure, or where things are getting bogged down. The HQQ is this, "What is the one question which, if answered, will enable me to move this negotiation forward?" It is an effective invitation to you and to your team to focus on the one thing that is causing a problem, so you can work on overcoming it.

85. How do you overcome the opposing party's preconceived prejudices?

Everybody has prejudices of one kind or another and, unless they are extreme, they aren't a particular problem. A prejudice is a deeply held conviction about something and, for you to notice it at all, it will be contrary to the way you think. It follows that the other side will believe you to be as prejudiced as you believe them to be.

"A belief is not merely an idea that the mind possesses; it is an idea that possesses the mind."
Robert Bolton

When thinking about how to overcome prejudices, your first consideration should be about whether you need to overcome them at all. If it isn't hindering the progress of the negotiation, but is just some point of view that you don't support, simply acknowledge that the view has been expressed and move on. If, however, it is impacting discussions, then it needs to be dealt with in some way.

Let's take an example relating to wine bottles. Imagine a wine merchant who is seeking to reduce costs, and improve the quality of the wine, by replacing traditional corks with screw tops. Scientifically speaking, screw top closures on wine bottles are superior to corks as a means of keeping the wine in the bottle fresh. However the potential buyer says, "I will never buy wine in screw top bottles because I don't like them and neither do my customers". How might you seek to overcome this prejudice?

Understanding why the buyer feels this way is a good place to start. On what evidence do they base their view? What do they know about the efficiency of screw tops? Do they understand that this is cheaper, and that some of this benefit can be passed on both to the buyer and to the end customer? Do they appreciate they might have to deal with fewer complaints about wine quality? What is that worth to them?

You also need to look at the issue from their point of view. Nothing is quite like the experience of pulling a cork from a bottle of wine and listening to the 'pop'. If a customer sees pulling the cork as part of their lifestyle, and a great thing to do in convivial company – that moment of anticipation before the wine is poured and tasted – then they won't easily give it up.

So, as the negotiator, perhaps you might acknowledge the prejudice, even though it's not based on science, and keep the corks – but ensure the extra cost is reflected in the price of your product.

86. Without insulting the negotiator, how do you find out their fallback position in the shortest time possible?

It can be more difficult than at first appears to insult a negotiator. Experienced negotiators have been in all sorts of situations and tend not to take things too personally – and in a professional negotiation things rarely become personal.

Finding the other party's fallback position quickly is desirable from an efficiency point of view, but isn't necessarily the best way to the best deal. Negotiators will expect the other party to work hard to extract concessions – and that cuts both ways. Would you give your bottom line positions away for nothing much? Undoubtedly not; why would you, unless there's something in it for you?

Therefore, the most obvious way to find out is to ask the question outright. However, the question, "What is your bottom line?" Or, "Is this your bottom line?" is not likely to reveal the truth.

If a quick deal is rarely the best deal, then how do you get to a conclusion in the quickest appropriate time? This is down to experience and good planning:

• Know your subject, and what deals are being done in similar circumstances elsewhere;
• Get to know who you are dealing with, and the kind of deals they have done with your company previously, or with other clients;
• Observe, through the course of the negotiation, how many times they are moving their position, and what the size of the movements is. If the frequency and size of position movements is decreasing, this may be because they are getting towards their bottom line. But be aware that this may also be a tactical ploy, and this is what they want you to think;
• Weigh up all the pros and cons – if time is more important to you for a particular reason, your best deal may indeed be a quick one. As long as you acknowledge to your own side that you are compromising on the possible terms of an agreement in order to do a quick deal, and that is acceptable, then fine.

87. How do you respond to so-called 'Hassle Free Deals' offered by the car salesperson, where no negotiation appears possible?

What possible variables other than price could I negotiate?

These 'hassle free deals' are very few and far between. Typically you will find this situation occurring where someone is producing a product which is scarce, in great demand, and they can therefore name their price. Hand-build luxury cars are a good example – if you don't buy one, somebody else will. Even in these circumstances, an experienced negotiator will ask themselves, "Well if I can't get anything off the price, what else can I get? Extras? More advantageous finance terms? Any servicing thrown in? What about a better trade-in price for my car?"

If you don't ask, you don't give the other party the opportunity to say yes. As a general rule, always be suspicious of any claim that negotiation isn't possible. It usually is.

88. How do you approach sealed bid tendering demanded over a major contract?

Sealed bid tendering can be unlike any other negotiation in the sense that you get one chance to put your best price in, and that's that. The best price wins.

However, there are things you can do to strengthen the likelihood of success. Some people who are running a sealed bid exercise, say to identify a provider of service under a contract to build something, are ruthlessly ethical, in that they will treat all potential bidders exactly the same. This is intended to ensure that all are playing on a level playing field.

This should not, however, deter you from asking questions that might help you. A gentle conversation with the right person at the right time can elicit even small details that may help you formulate your own bid – the kind of profit margin that they expect you to make; the number of bidders; whether anyone has yet lodged a bid; the kind of range in which they might expect the bids to be; details of any similar previous exercises that have been run.

If you are able to get any information in this way, take all available steps to challenge it by researching the broad issues, and seeing if other people will confirm what you have been told. Be aware that people may well be employing tactics to get you to raise the level of your bid – by suggesting prices will be at a certain level, or suggesting there is more interest than there actually is. They will be trying to balance their desire to influence your thinking with a need to avoid frightening you off.

The second area where you can help yourself is to make your bid as attractive as possible. This isn't simply about money. Include details about aspects that will be of assistance to the other party – quality standards; any compensation arrangements you might offer for non-compliance with any terms in the contract, remembering that substantial compensation offered will convey a sense that you will deliver on the contract, because you clearly wouldn't wish to pay any compensation; and commitments around meeting key deadlines and where you can actually improve on them in areas that your competitors cannot.

How could I make my bid as attractive as possible?

Research your competitors, and those who you think may be interested in bidding, carefully. Watch particularly for potential bidders who really need the work, say because their current activity is coming to an end. They may be prepared to bid extremely favourably simply to keep their business ticking over whilst they work to obtain more lucrative contracts.

Calculate your sums very carefully – there is no point in winning a bid and obtaining work that is of no value to you.

Bids are generally considered in the round, rather than simply on the price. The more that you can put in that is attractive, and the keener your price, the greater your chances of success.

89. How do you respond to elements of a deal which are labelled by the other side as 'non-negotiable'?

It is common in negotiations for each side to have certain issues on which they are unwilling or unable to move – perhaps because they are extremely important, or are points of principle which are of particular significance for some reason.

Through discussion, work out firstly whether an issue is genuinely non-negotiable, or whether this is a tactical ploy intended to get a substantial concession from you before movement can be made. Consider upfront whether the matter that is described as non-negotiable is important to you or not. If it is something that you can accept, then you will often be able to achieve movement from the other side by agreeing not to pursue the matter further. When presented with a so-called non-negotiable in this way, seek to enhance its value to you as a bargaining chip by saying that it is very important to your side that movement is achieved on this issue.

**"The freedom of the city is not negotiable. We cannot negotiate with those who say, 'What's mine is mine and what's yours is negotiable'."
John F. Kennedy**

Clearly the greatest difficulty will occur for you when something is genuinely non-negotiable, but you need it to become negotiable. Most things become negotiable if the terms offered are right, although this can be a very expensive way of doing business. Equally, matters which are genuinely non-negotiable might become negotiable later if movement is made on other aspects of the deal which change the circumstances. Or something which is non-negotiable at one time may become negotiable at another time, because pressures on the other side which you are not aware of have changed.

Never accept that something is non-negotiable without working to understand why that is the case. In finding this out, a solution may well present itself.

Seek to understand their Reason Why.

90. How do you develop the skill, the vocabulary or the backing to concentrate on 'issues' rather than 'positions' when negotiating?

We have previously considered the difference between a negotiating position and a lie – a negotiating position is something which might not actually be true, but it is part of the negotiation. As negotiators understand the rules, this is really all part of the game. Negotiating positions are an integral part of any negotiation, and without them it wouldn't be a negotiation at all.

See chapter 46.

Therefore, you have to go through the negotiation to understand the true issues such as the other party's bottom line. There is no magic formula for getting there. However, if you have prepared fully for the discussion, you and your team understand your respective roles, and you all firmly understand and have a single view of your goals, then you will already have achieved all the buy-in you need from your own people. As for the vocabulary, that's rather more straightforward. Remembering that any negotiation is essentially a collaborative effort between people with a view to reaching a mutually satisfactory outcome, a negotiation is nothing more than a structured conversation between interested parties.

The skills needed are rooted in common sense, and involve the application of the tools and techniques we have looked at in this book. The more they are practised in discussion between your team, and then in a live environment, the better. However there is no substitute for watching a more experienced negotiator at work and, through understanding all of the points in this book, appreciating the subtleties of what they are doing and why they are doing it.

91. How do you make best use of your relationships and your personality in a negotiation?

Great negotiators recognise and appreciate that negotiation is a people business and that their chances of reaching a really good outcome are enhanced if they understand what makes the people around the table tick – and that applies as much to the people on their own side of the table as it does to others.

Equally, great negotiators will build relationships with people whenever they can, because when they need to rely on those relationships they won't have time to build them. One of the key Go MAD Thinking Principles is about involving others who might be able to help you. Ask yourself the question, "Who do I know who may be able to help me in the future, even if they can't help me now?" Develop mutually beneficial relationships with those people with the same energy that you would devote to developing a relationship with someone who could help you tomorrow.

> **"In my relationships with persons I have found that it does not help, in the long run, to act as though I were something that I am not."**
> **Carl Rogers**

Using your personality as a negotiator is important. The 'human touch' in an essentially human interaction is very important, and the line of least effort is to simply be yourself. If you are attempting to cultivate an image that does not represent the person you truly are, then you are inevitably bound to fail, because your guard will fall, and the things you really stand for will shine through. Use your humour – it makes you more personable, more approachable, and more fun to deal with – and we all like to enjoy what we do so injecting a little fun into negotiations, no matter how important they are, is always worthwhile. It's all a question of balance – nobody wants to be confronted by a clown except at a circus.

> **"Two cannibals eating a clown.**
> **One says to the other:**
> **'Does this taste funny to you?' "**
> **Tommy Cooper**

92. How important is integrity to a negotiator?

It really is true that a negotiator who has no integrity has nothing. People you negotiate with need to know that you are good for your word, and that you can be trusted. Trust takes time to build up, and no time at all to destroy. Guard your integrity and reputation jealously as it is your greatest asset, more important even than your experience. An inexperienced negotiator with integrity will get much further than an experienced negotiator who has lost theirs.

Think of people you know. Do you like to deal with people of low integrity? Will you go out of your way to help them, or will you do the least possible? Then consider, honestly, what people might say about you. Are you the kind of person you want to be? What do you stand for?

How do I demonstrate my integrity?

In a negotiation, integrity is easy to demonstrate, and it will help you to achieve great results. Lack of integrity is difficult to cover up, and it will stop you from achieving the best deals. You might still reach agreements, but they won't be the best you could have done. This is because people with whom you are negotiating will hold things back as a contingency that you will let them down, because they don't trust you to deliver fully, properly, or at all on your part of the bargain.

93. How important is it to establish and build a rapport or connection with the people you are negotiating with, and what techniques do you use to achieve that?

If you can see the good in people (and even difficult people have their good qualities) then it becomes easier to build rapport. Human beings are essentially a social animal and rapport building therefore becomes natural. People who are the most difficult to forge relationships with are usually those who hold back, against their natural inclination, perhaps because they fear that if they let you in too close then you will take advantage of them.

How could I possibly build greater rapport?

There are a number of useful techniques for building rapport, and these apply regardless of who you are looking to build rapport with:

• Make time to build relationships when you and they are not under particular pressure;
• Consider whether it is appropriate to use social time

to do this – perhaps before or after meetings, or quite separate from work;

- Find out what is important to them, both in a work sense, and more widely. Get to know things about issues that matter to them, so that you can converse properly;
- Do more listening than talking, at least in the early stages of a relationship. Pay attention to them, and show them that you are interested by asking pertinent questions and by checking your understanding of things said;
- Share information about yourself. This is not going to put you at a disadvantage in a negotiation;
- Turn your mobile phone to silent when you are with people – interruptions can be extremely annoying. If you are expecting an important call, say so when you meet. It's courteous, and helps to set expectations, as well as showing that you are aware that it's not just you who will be interrupted;
- In the negotiations themselves, remember the courtesies at the front of the meeting – introducing people who have not met before; ensuring people are given refreshments; checking the time people need to be away and so on.

It's often the little things that count – if you show you are interested in people, people are more likely to be interested in you.

94. How do you find out about the other person's real need to take your product?

Almost without exception, if someone has turned up to negotiate with you, they are interested in your product – at the very least to find out more about it, if not to buy it. And if the former, it's a sure bet that they are comparing your product, its features and benefits, and the terms of a potential deal, with those offered by your competitors.

Therefore, careful preparation before the negotiation will involve looking at the wider marketplace and the kind of deals that are being done elsewhere, and careful research to understand the people who are coming to talk to you. The more you can find out about them, the more likely you are going to be able to fulfil their particular needs. Perhaps they are looking to fulfil a particularly large order, and they need multiple suppliers. Or they may have been let down by a regular supplier and need your product quickly, and almost at any price. If they are making cars but have no headlights, they can't sell the car!

"Information is the negotiator's greatest weapon."
Victor Kiam

Never believe anything they say about what your competitors are offering; great negotiators love to play one party off against another. The important thing to do is to keep your team firmly focused on your negotiating brief, and not to be diverted from your goal. Be aware that the other team may tell you that they have almost signed a deal with someone else. A deal that is not finalised is not a deal, so things are still negotiable – otherwise they wouldn't be wasting their time with you. So consider carefully whether they are using a tactic, or whether this really is the last opportunity for you to steal a deal from under someone else's nose.

95. How do you help others to 'sell' the deal to their own side?

It is always worthwhile to expend effort in helping the other negotiators – as well as helping to achieve a deal in the first place, it helps to build long-term profitable relationships, and it makes you easier to deal with. People will always choose to deal with people who make their lives easier in some way, and that can work powerfully to your advantage. Negotiators will often accept a deal that is less favourable in terms of overall price if they are absolutely confident that the other party will deliver on their commitments, on time, and without problems. Certainty of supply of products is vital to business survival, especially in a world where it is considered uneconomic to carry large backup supplies of goods, components or materials.

You can help people to sell to their own side by emphasising repeatedly the beneficial aspects to them of the deal you are offering. This is easiest when you understand their needs, and that is achieved by discussing their situation in as much detail as you need to in order to understand what is important to them. This cuts both ways, and it is important therefore to ensure that they understand the same about you.

It follows that if they perceive you to be helpful to them, then they will return the courtesy, either now or when you really need it. And it's easy to be helpful – you will already know why you think they should be reaching agreement with you, because you will have covered it in your possibility thinking at the time of your preparation.

96. How do you know when to shut up?

You've heard the saying, "Quit while you're ahead"? Well, in negotiations, don't! Otherwise the other party may catch up. If you are ahead, stay ahead, and close the deal on the most advantageous terms you can get, whilst preserving any relationship you need to keep for the next time you negotiate with the same people or organisation.

Now consider this against that other saying; "If your words are no better than silence, then remain silent". Or, "Say nothing if you have nothing to say". Do these help us in negotiations?

Frankly, no. Negotiations are conversations between people. If they are going well, you will carry on until the deal is concluded. If they are not going well, you need to find a way through the impasse, and this will be achieved through further conversation – with your own side in or out of the room, and with the other team, either formally or informally, in the meeting, or in the corridor in an adjournment.

**"Never forget the power of silence,
that massively disconcerting pause which goes on
and on and may at last induce an opponent to
babble and backtrack nervously."
Lance Morrow**

So, when do you shut up? When you've made your point, you have confirmed that it has been properly understood, and you are waiting for a response. Then silence can become a potent weapon. Wait for the other party to respond. Leave them time to think. Let the ensuing silence put pressure on them. Fight the urge to say something – we often feel that silences are there to be broken. Interject only to reconfirm that your point is understood or your question is clear. Don't let the other negotiators off the hook by answering for them.

97. How many people can one person negotiate with and stand a chance of winning?

Provided you follow the tools and techniques for each of the three stages of negotiation there should be no difficulty in achieving satisfactory results in your negotiations.

The number of people on the other team is irrelevant. This is particularly so when you consider the roles which each are playing; typically there will only be at most four or five people who take an active role in the discussions. Others are there to contribute to particular issues, or because the politics of the situation demand they are there. It is straightforward to identify who the key players are on the other team simply by watching the body language, and by seeing how other people on that team react when someone is speaking. Close observation will tell you whether they are key or not.

Careful preparation before the negotiation will involve finding out all you can about the people on the other team, and in particular who the leaders and decision takers are, as well as those who have influence even though their job title may not suggest it. These are the people to concentrate on, whilst of course treating everyone on the other team with respect regardless of status.

98. What is the ideal personality type for conducting successful negotiations?

In short, there isn't one. It doesn't matter whether you are extrovert, introvert, affiliative, or naturally reserved. It is not personality type which determines a great negotiator, rather it is the degree to which certain key attributes are developed – and the best news is that these attributes can indeed all be developed, as long as you have a strong enough Reason Why:

Which attributes could I further develop?

- An interest in people, and what makes them tick;
- The passion to do a great job;
- An ability to think clearly, and to follow a systematic approach to the three stages of negotiation;
- An ability to clearly communicate ideas and concepts,

185

and to argue in favour of the benefits of a particular course of action;

- The patience to work with people who may be less capable than you in some respects;
- The humility to work with people who are more capable than you in others;
- A strong sense of self-awareness so you know how you come across to others. This then enables you to make appropriate adjustments to your style.
- Attention to detail;
- A preparedness to see things through to the end;
- And, often, a competitive streak. This can be wholly internal to the individual, or on display for all to see, but usually it will be there somewhere.

A good team will have a cross-section of people with well developed abilities in some or all of these areas. A great negotiator can recognise qualities in people, assemble teams that fulfil the requirements of the job, and motivate people to give their best.

99. How can the facilitator set the mood to acquire the best responses from those involved?

Building the right mood in a meeting is important, whether it is a meeting of your team, or the negotiation itself.

In terms of managing your own team, and bringing out the best in them as individuals and as team players, it is useful to get the right mix of people in the first place. Giving room for people to get to know each other as individual people and not just simply as work colleagues is an important element in building effective teams which is sometimes overlooked, often because of time constraints. However make time for this activity – it will pay back dividends.

> **"One of the things I learned when I was negotiating was that until I changed myself I could not change others."**
> **Nelson Mandela**

Great lead negotiators lead from the front, and demonstrate the kind of behaviours they expect from others in the team. Taking time to listen to alternative points of view is going to lead to better results when you engage in possibility thinking, because people will not be reticent about coming out with ideas that are off the wall. Even patently 'daft' ideas can spark the thoughts that lead to a conclusion, so in possibility thinking the degree to which people feel comfortable to contribute fully is vital. Otherwise people will naturally go for the 'safe' option; thinking will follow traditional lines appropriate to the culture of your organisation, and little if any new thinking will emerge.

We have looked at how you can manage the mood within meetings in chapter 64. Simple techniques, applied effectively, will create the best environment for all parties to a negotiation to come out with the best solution.

100. What do you look for in terms of body language and verbal responses?

Most communication is non-verbal. Of course it is vital to listen to what is being said, but it is always informative to look for how it is being said in terms of intonation and body language. Equally, you gain a lot from watching how others react to things that are said to you. If someone on the other team is saying something that others don't agree with, they will look down, look away, lean away from the person speaking, fold their arms defensively, or just look disinterested.

Body language is a field in itself. However look for the following tell-tale signs:

*   Does the speaker look you in the eye when they speak? If not, they may be lying;
*   Does the speaker look at you intently? Again, they may be trying to convince you too strongly about something they don't expect you to agree to;
*   Are gestures aggressive? This can signify nerves, such as when someone isn't comfortable with what they are saying, or if they are at a part of the negotiation which is really important for them but they don't want you to know it;
*   Are people smiling? If so, what are they happy about? Have you just given away a concession that was really important to them? In which case, make sure you get something valuable in exchange;
*   Do people on the other side of the table look comfortable with each other? If not, they may not all be pursuing the same goal. Consider how you could use that knowledge to your advantage;
*   Do people look tired? Tired people don't think well, and this could either present you with an opportunity to press for a better deal, or could prevent you from reaching one, for instance because they become intransigent.

What will others conclude from observing my body language?

When considering body language, remember that it works both ways. Experienced people on the other team will be watching you carefully. Take care to present an engaged, attentive persona, whilst hiding emotions that might give your true position away. This isn't about being poker faced and hiding your personality, it's more about showing just the right things.

Take care also to ensure your team watch their own body language. Help each other by pointing out, perhaps with a

188

subtle note, anything that causes you concern, and encourage your people to help you in the same way.

101. How do you build trust?

Perhaps not so surprisingly, building trust between negotiators involves the same steps as building trust in any relationship. The difference in a relationship between negotiators as opposed, say, to a personal or family relationship, is that the thing you have in common is your role. The role of a negotiator involves complying with a certain set of unwritten rules, at least to some degree:

* You both know that you are there to do the best you can for yourself, your company or your cause;
* You both know that if you get something in a negotiation, for instance a really good price, then the money you get has to come from somewhere, and you can't both have it all;
* You both know that it's okay to take a position in negotiations and argue that you can't possibly move off it, even though that's not true;
* You both know that long-term, profitable relationships involve both parties getting something they want through the negotiation – the so-called 'win:win' scenario;
* You both know that if it is a genuinely one-off negotiation, then each will be out to drive an extremely hard bargain, even to the point where the personal side of things can almost break down.

Assuming that the negotiation isn't a one-off, better relationships between negotiators will lead to better deals, and trust is the key element. In order to build trust you need to:

How do I build trust?

- Demonstrate that you have a robust and positive set of personal values, and that you will defend them – i.e. you stand for something;
- Show you have personal integrity and are good for your word – when you say you will do something, you deliver;
- Illustrate, through what you say and do and how you do it, that you are interested in the human side of a negotiation – that you can communicate with people, and that you care about the impact of events on them.

These are not qualities that a negotiator can easily pretend to have when they don't. The image you choose to portray is important, and the nearer that is to the 'real you', the easier it is. Consider what you would want as the ideal negotiator sitting across the table from you against the checklist above. Then consider whether this is what people see in you.

Trust is a great asset. Never let anyone persuade you to ruin a trusting relationship for what will almost inevitably be short-term gain. It is one of your most powerful and effective tools. Think of someone you know who is generally distrusted, and question how they would fare as a negotiator. Not well.

102. When aiming to build a working relationship with someone new to your business who sees you as a 'rival', how do you negotiate with them in order to agree or compromise on how the relationship should work going forward? (Note: that this negotiation is made all the more difficult if one party uses open communication while the new employee 'hoards' information.)

New people onto a team or into an organisation need to

find their feet, and sometimes we forget just how daunting it can be to come into a new situation – everyone seems to know everybody and everything, you feel at a disadvantage in almost every conversation, and you know that everyone is looking at you to see what you're worth, whether you were a good hire, and whether they are going to like you and like working with you. Often there are politics flying around as well – some may see the new person as a threat, some may not even approve of the job at all, some may have applied for it and not got it.

Before going in with all guns blazing, therefore, it is always worthwhile to take a breath and see how things pan out over the first few weeks, whilst doing your best to give the benefit of the doubt and to build a trusting relationship.

If things don't come right with a little effort on both sides, then treat the situation as a negotiation – your objective is to influence the thinking of the other party to your point of view on how the relationship should be, going forward. Consider the possibilities available to you; apply the key principles of the Go MAD Thinking System, and carry out some parallel thinking to consider matters from their point of view.

Troublesome working relationships, where there is conflict between people, have three overriding features:
1.   They are sub-optimal from a business efficiency point of view;
2.   They always have an underlying cause;
3.   And they are no fun.

Finding the cause leads to the way to fix it. Being efficient in your roles, and enjoying what you do, should provide a strong enough Reason Why to address the issue.

**"We must sail sometimes with the wind and
sometimes against it, – but we must sail,
and not drift, nor lie at anchor."
Oliver Wendell Holmes**

Waiting for someone else to come along and resolve
things is rarely a smart, or particularly pleasant, option, so
avoid it.

103. **"Whatever they say, no one ever opens their
books to another party!" So, are 'partnering
deals' – i.e. where one party confers favoured
status on another – just another and more
elaborate ploy to gain advantage? If yes, how
do you make it work for you? If no, then how
do you make partnerships in negotiating work
for you?**

Negotiators should only enter into a partnership
arrangement – which involves, for example, the conferring
of exclusivity on one person or organisation for a period
of time – if there is distinct advantage to be gained through
such an arrangement. Consider what those advantages
might be:

• The gaining of guaranteed access to the products or
  services of a supplier, or access to a sales market,
  which gives you stability of some kind – cash flow,
  revenues, production time-scales and the like;
• The ability to work with a partner who understands
  your business needs extremely well, and vice versa;
• An arrangement which precludes the partner
  organisation from working with certain of your
  competitors, bearing in mind that there are certain
  aspects of competition law which need to be complied
  with, and these differ in different countries;

- Early and preferential access to new products or services from the partner, or new markets developed by the partner.

It is always sensible to take certain precautions in this situation, based on common sense – don't keep all of your eggs in one basket and become so reliant on a partner that your business success, or even survival, is reliant on theirs; re-tender from time to time, and keep an eye on the wider market, to ensure that a long-term relationship is still as commercially viable as you would like, and that the terms continue to compare favourably with those available elsewhere.

No matter how close the relationship, any deal you seek to achieve with a potential partner is a negotiation like any other – they will be seeking to get the best terms for themselves, just as you will. Even in a win:win situation, the wins do not have to be equal.

104. How do you remain solution focused under pressure, or when the negotiation is going off at a tangent?

One way of staying solution focused is to ensure that you focus clearly on your goal. Your goal, or goals, should be written, clear and unambiguous, and you should invest the time at the planning stage to ensure that your wider team understand and are committed to the negotiating objectives.

Refer to the goal frequently. Keep a copy of it with you, so that you can mentally (or actually) tick off each element as you achieve it. This will ensure nothing is missed. Remember that pressure is a feeling that is your reaction to a situation; intense pressure can weaken your ability to think clearly, and this in turn reduces your effectiveness as a negotiator. So if pressures are becoming a problem, take steps to reduce them. Take time out through an adjournment, or increase the options available to you through an individual or team possibility thinking exercise.

"The pressure of adversity does not affect the mind of a brave man... It is more powerful than external circumstances."
Seneca

Become consciously aware of your four thinking components and check whether they are helpful or hindering. If the latter, then start talking internally to yourself in a helpful way and ask HQQs to help focus your mind on solutions.

If the negotiation appears to be going off at a tangent, a solution focused approach is to ask yourself, "What could I possibly do to get it back on track?" Always think possibilities.

105. How do you identify when to walk away from a negotiation?

Experienced negotiators will only ever walk away from a negotiation in the following circumstances:

- They know that no deal is available on terms that they will find acceptable, having tried all of the options that are available to them;
- They believe a deal is available, and are prepared to walk away from the negotiating table as a tactical ploy to force a change of mood or position from the other side – but they'll recognise the risks associated with this course of action because, having walked away, there can never be a guarantee of a way back;
- They don't need the deal.

194

In business life potential deals do fall over for a whole raft of reasons – the terms are unacceptable, or political considerations are preventing agreement, or there are serious misgivings about the other party's ability to deliver. Bearing in mind the amount of energy, time and money that will have been invested in preparing for, and then conducting, the negotiations, it is always worth going that extra mile to see if some potential breakthrough has been overlooked.

"Never cut what you can untie."
Joseph Joubert

It is generally a good idea to attempt to keep the door open so that negotiations can be reconvened if some new situation develops, and you never know when you might run into these people again. So keep your options open for as long as possible. Close the door gently – don't slam it!

106. How do you walk away from a negotiation without feeling let down or disappointed?

Any negotiator will feel a degree of frustration at failing to reach an agreement. This is perfectly natural. Nobody likes to lose, and the opposite of a win:win has to involve losing in some way, for both parties.

However, there is nothing that cannot be turned to advantage, and at the very least every negotiation is good experience for your own team. You should also make a point of carrying out the third stage in negotiations even if no deal has been reached. This involves thinking following the negotiation, both individually and as a team, to look at what went well and what went not so well. As long as these lessons are learned and then put into practice at the next available opportunity then all of the effort has not been entirely wasted.

**"Life is a series of lessons which
must be lived to be understood."
Ralph Waldo Emerson**

---

107. What is a win:win outcome, and is it possible?

All of the best negotiating outcomes involve an element of advantage for each side – the so-called win:win where everyone gets at least some of what they came for. There are a few points to emphasise around wins:

- They are rarely equal. One party will be nearer to their ideal end position than the other. Precisely where you end up is down to the skills and persistence of the respective negotiators;
- Outcomes can be different every time even though the subject matter might be identical; just because you paid £2 a widget last week doesn't mean you have to achieve the same deal this week. A whole range of factors may have changed since then, including your own desire to drive an even better deal this time;
- Remembering that negotiating is about influencing the thinking of others, people are strongly influenced by their own vision of success – so take time to engage the imagination of the other team to help them focus on what success may look like for them. Paint pictures that are vivid – pay attention to the saying, "If you can touch it or taste it you're more likely to buy it".

**"My Father said; 'You must never try to make all
the money that's in a deal. Let the other fellow
make some money too, because if you have a
reputation for always making all the money, you
won't have many deals'."
J. Paul Getty**

---

108. What is the difference in process used if you are negotiating on a personal basis to that on a company basis?

In a word – emotion. Negotiations that you carry out on a personal basis are, in process terms, no different from any other negotiation. However, if you are buying a fleet of cars for an organisation there is likely to be less emotional energy invested in the purchase than if you are buying a car for yourself.

Studies show that the perceived value of a company's money is around a third of the value of your own money. This, if you let it, will impact on your thinking, and on the effectiveness of your negotiation.

The best way to do the best deals, therefore, is to treat someone else's money as if it were your own, and to treat your personal negotiations as if they were organisational ones. This gives two distinct advantages to you:

* People will see very powerfully that you are serious about the money side of a potential deal, and that you are firmly focused on the financial implications;
* In your personal negotiations, you will come across to the other party with greater conviction that you are there to do a deal, but only on the right terms.

Imagine you are going to buy a house. You and your family are dead set on a particular house, and you are prepared to pay the full asking price for the house just to get it.

As the buyer, your best tactic is to give the impression that you are undecided between this house and another one, and that issues like the speed the deal could go through (even if you're prepared to wait months) and the price will be the deciding factors. Looking and acting as if you want to move in tomorrow isn't going to get you the best deal.

As the seller, your best tactic is to give the impression that your house is really popular, and that you expect to sell it within days. In reality, you might be desperate to sell because you have already found somewhere you want to move to, and so for you speed may be more important than price to some extent.

Underneath, emotions on both sides will be running high. However, the fact that you are there at all means you might be prepared to buy, and they might be prepared to sell. The rest is essentially just detail.

So, the person who stays as dispassionate as possible will be likely to get nearest to their ideal position.

However, as the buyer, it is easy to have hindering thoughts and ask low quality questions that engage your imagination in a way that puts more pressure on you. For example, "What if there really are loads of people who want to buy this house, and how would I feel if I lost it just for the sake of a few thousand pounds?"

Adopting a more helpful solution focused approach, you could ask higher quality questions including, "What are the possible risks and implications I need to consider?" Or, "What is the value of the deal to me in totality, not just in terms of the bottom line price?" You should be aware of the impact of your own emotions, and those of the people close to you, when negotiating in a personal situation, and recognise that they should be considered alongside every other aspect of the deal. In the end, they will influence you only to the extent that you let them!

109. Some union representatives see negotiation as a bit of a game, where they have to go through the motions but know that it may be futile; how should this be handled?

Negotiations with unions are, to all intents and purposes, the same as any other negotiation: both parties come to the table wanting something. However, consider the following points:

- Negotiations may be about intangible rather than tangible things – proposed changes to working practices are less tangible than a physical product. But anything that impacts people will be seen as having a benefit, or a cost, associated with it;
- A union may wish an employer to start doing something, or to stop doing something, which is nothing to do with money; for example, to start giving people two weeks notice of changes to shift patterns instead of one week;
- A pay negotiation involves an employer paying out money in exchange for acceptance by employees – at its extreme, people will carry on doing what they did before provided the employer pays more. Otherwise they'll stop work. So, what each party is putting into the deal is denominated in a different currency.

Why these factors are important is that in negotiations of this kind, a union is typically negotiating on the basis of what its officials believe is in the interests of a range of different parties:

Parallel thinking – consider possible implications for others.

- Its members in the organisation;
- Its members in different organisations who aren't directly involved. E.g. a lucrative pay deal in one place can have an impact on pay talks elsewhere;
- The wider interests of the union: if it achieves a good outcome, more people may join, bringing in more subscriptions;
- Kudos flowing to officials who achieve a deal which is perceived both within and outside their organisation to be good may have wider political implications,

perhaps giving them greater credibility in the eyes of people they are seeking to influence on other matters of importance to them, or for their careers;

• Other employers may be watching carefully with the intention of following suit.

Thus, there can be significant pressures both inside and outside the organisation which need to be considered by both parties. This inevitably leads to complication.

Ultimately, however, the rules of the negotiation are the same as any other, as are the stages of negotiation. The negotiation will only become futile, or will break down, because the needs of one or more of the parties are not viewed as having been met.

As a general rule it is always worth bearing in mind that if two parties freely enter into a negotiation, both are there because they believe that there is a deal to be had.

A helpful self-talk statement.

110. The film 'The 'Negotiator' was excellent in providing insight into negotiating in a hostage situation, as the stakes are clearly higher; does this mean the tactics have to be different?

Learning how to negotiate in any situation involves gaining familiarity and, with experience, mastery of a generic skill set. In other words, there is little difference between a small negotiation involving a deal worth a few hundred pounds and huge negotiation involving millions – or, indeed, a negotiation involving the release of a hostage and the saving of someone's life. The point is that the skills used are the same, even if the outputs aren't.

Clearly, there will inevitably be greater pressures on the negotiators if there is more at stake – and there are no higher stakes than life or death. Therefore, professional hostage negotiators are expert at building relationships with people who are under incredible strain, and who as a result may not be thinking or acting rationally. Equally, they have to strongly develop their ability to conceal their own emotions – because the more pressure you put on yourself in a negotiation, the weaker your ability to think clearly and logically.

"The most important single ingredient in the formula of success is knowing how to get along with people."
Theodore Roosevelt

Hostage negotiators will go to great lengths to create a bond of trust with the people they are negotiating with. This is about building an environment for the negotiations which is as calm as possible, and where potential threats are minimised. In this situation, there is more emphasis on establishing the right circumstances in which the negotiation can take place than you would normally find in a commercial negotiation.

111. How do you get the maximum buy-in to the end result before you have to go through all the games that people play in negotiations?

To the inexperienced negotiator, the process of negotiating can indeed look like a game. You will often hear people say, "But everyone knows where this negotiation is going to end up – why can't they just get on with it?" I invite you to consider an old adage: "A quick deal is rarely the best deal". This is true. Consider two parties in a pay negotiation. The employee representatives put in a claim for a 6% pay rise for everyone. You could settle that pay negotiation at the first meeting by offering 6%.

A quick deal is rarely the best deal.

201

But if you did, let's consider the possible risks and implications:

- The other party will think you are weak, or desperate;
- They may ask for other concessions, such as more holidays, or a shorter working week – things that will cost you money, and which may make you look inflexible if you then refuse. One thing is for sure – the other party will not thank you for your generosity, and just take the 6%. Life doesn't work like that;
- And if they do take the 6% with good grace and walk away, what will happen at your next negotiation with the employee representatives, regardless of the subject matter? They will expect instant agreement, and their claims will increase;
- Next year's pay claim will be for 9%. If they got 6% with no argument, why not ask for more? Maybe they won't wait a year. They could be back for more in six months.

Negotiations are about influencing the thinking of others, and achieving wherever possible some mutual benefit – the so-called win:win. But the relative size of your win compared to the win on the other side is where the time is spent to good effect. The negotiating game is about preparing your position, and carrying out the negotiations through to conclusion in a manner which maximises the tangible and intangible benefits to you. That takes time.

112. If you could cut the time available for negotiations in half, what key elements would you need to focus on in the negotiations and how do you influence people to do that?

Bearing in mind that a quick deal is rarely the best deal, if time is absolutely of the essence, then consider the following:

- If you make it known to the other team that time is really important to you, then they will use this as a weapon against you. If you were negotiating against someone, and you believed they were under real time pressure, then you would adopt a tactic of sitting on your hands to see how many concessions they would make, without you giving anything much in return, simply because they are under time pressure. Therefore, if the tables are turned, and it is you who is under time pressure, don't reveal this to them;

possible risks and implications

- Instead, work to demonstrate some advantage to them of coming to an agreement with you more quickly, whilst hiding the fact that you are in a hurry. If you are selling a product, for instance, say that you have an unexpected surplus due to cancellation of a previous order, and these may be available although there are other interested parties. Suggest that this is a deal that may only be available for a limited time – otherwise you'll continue the negotiation but it won't be on the same terms. In this situation, you are seeking to engage the imagination of the other party to envisage the benefit to them of a quick deal without declaring that your real motivation is that you are in a hurry.

Influencing one of the four thinking components.

There are circumstances in which a quick deal can be the best for you. By way of example, if your company is in dire need of immediate revenue, perhaps because you need to meet payment on supplies or salaries, then closing a deal at very little profit but with immediate payment terms may be better for you because it's cheaper than taking credit from a bank. However you can't run a business in this way long-term; as long as you know what you are doing, and why, and are clear about your longer-term strategy and business requirements, then the occasional quick deal can be highly beneficial.

Equally, if you are seeking to establish a presence in a new market, and it is important to build a credible position quickly, then a few quick deals may be a good investment, perhaps to buy market share at the expense of immediate profit. Bear in mind the implications – because sooner or later you need to make a profit, and that might mean increasing prices. Alternatively, increasing output will reduce unit costs and if your planning has been carried out thoughtfully then you will know what output to achieve in order to make profit in due course.

113. What is your BATNA? (Best Alternative To A Negotiated Agreement)

This is a little bit of negotiators' slang you may come across from time to time. If, at the apparent end of a negotiation, there is no agreement, there are various options available to you:

- Call it a day and walk away with no agreement;
- Seek to recommence the negotiations, by shifting your position, inviting the other party to shift theirs, or by introducing something new into the negotiation which may make an outcome more attractive to both parties;
- Walk away, but agree to reconsider the matter say in a month or three months. Time often changes the perspective of one or both sides;
- Adjourn the negotiation, and carry out detailed possibility thinking with your own team to determine whether you have overlooked any features of the negotiation which you can turn to your advantage;
- Assess whether the threat of ending a hitherto mutually profitable relationship will have a positive result – sometimes this may force people back to the negotiating table, but it's a high risk strategy because you just might lose the relationship, and so you need to be certain you can live without it in the longer-term.

possible risks and implications

204

A deal which reaches agreement even on terms which are not favourable to one or the other of the parties – or both - is still a negotiated settlement. However, in these circumstances spend time and effort to put together a better outcome in the next deal, or risk long-term damage to the relationship, and to potential future business that may flow from it.

114. Anyone involved in a business deal or an employee relations negotiation is also a 'representative' of their company, or their union. How is this likely to affect their thinking, their negotiating and their assessment of what is a satisfactory finish?

In any negotiation, the respective negotiators are there to get the best deal they can for themselves and their organisation. For each individual, the term 'best' will generally mean a number of things:

*   A deal that they consider to be good;
*   A deal which they think others in their organisation will also think is good;
*   In the case of employee representatives, the representatives need to be able to 'sell' the deal to those they represent, as well as to people (and possibly committees) within the union itself;
*   Commercial negotiators are also often interested in their own reputation beyond their own team and their own organisation – for instance their contacts in industry networking groups and employers federations.

Skilled negotiators will seek to understand the various motivations that impact individuals on the other team – most especially those of the key people whose opinions really matter in terms of achieving the deal. This is where parallel thinking really pays dividends – seeking to get under the skin of the other players and see things from their point of view.

"Today is a new day. You will get out of it just what you put into it."
Mary Pickford

Always be wary of people who use the sometimes highly effective tactic of blaming their organisation: "I think this is a pretty good deal personally but I'd never get it through my people". Recognise that this is nothing but a tactic. Often the people referred to have no idea of the detail of what is going on in the negotiation at this stage, and have certainly not been consulted as to what their opinion is. The tactic can easily be overcome by responding along the lines of: "That's a real shame because this is the best I can do. Maybe I should talk to your people direct". Very rarely will you find that you have to. And if you do have to, well so much the better – then you're dealing with the real decision takers, not the warm-up act.

115. The balance of power between the parties is rarely equal. So, what strategy should you adopt if you are the weaker party? What if you are the stronger?

Who determines the strength of the parties? Strength, and weakness, is as much to do with perception as it is with reality. The fact that you are in the room with the other party means that you both want a deal. We have seen that a negotiation is fundamentally a collaborative exercise between parties who wish to reach an outcome, and who respect that there has to be mutual benefit to both parties. If there is no benefit to one or the other parties, or to both, then generally there will be no deal.

Therefore, do not assume that you are weak – or indeed that you are strong. However:

*   Use the Go MAD Thinking System to identify the strength of your Reason Why, the clarity of your Goal, and the strength of your Self-Belief. These are all areas that you can work on to improve, both at an individual level, and with your team;
*   As you get into the negotiation, use the same techniques to identify the situation on the other team; If you feel that they are in a better position than you, then carry out a possibility thinking exercise to identify measures that you can take to correct the situation;
*   Remember that you can observe low levels of confidence in other people through body language, through what they say, and how they say it – and this applies equally in reverse.

"The discovery of more is often blocked by the assumption of less."
Andy Gilbert

There are circumstances in which you will feel at a disadvantage – perhaps because you genuinely have a low level of expectation that you will be able to achieve a satisfactory outcome, or because you are genuinely desperate for a deal and you believe the other party are much more relaxed about it. This is where it becomes all the more important to clarify in your mind what your goal is. By focusing yourself, and your team, on the goal rather than on the incidental pressures that might otherwise affect you, you maximise the probability of a successful outcome.

116. What guidelines would you work to when negotiating with another party – in English – where this is not their first language?

There are two issues to consider:
- Firstly, and obviously, language;
- Secondly, and vitally, culture.

Language may indeed sound obvious, and there are some equally obvious rules to adopt:

- Speak clearly, and slowly, and spend time to check that people have understood what it is you are saying.
- Summarise often – it won't come across as patronising and it will be appreciated;
- Remember that different people on the other team will have different levels of competency in English – so take time to identify the person with the lowest level of English, and show patience when the other team take time out to explain matters in their native language;
- Take time to ensure you understand what it is the other team are saying to you. If you don't think you understand, ask them to repeat. Put it in your own words and play it back. Do this as often as is necessary – there is no point in moving the negotiation down a blind alley because neither party fully understands the other;
- Take more time out to give each party a rest – concentrating on a language which is not your own is mentally and physically draining. Show you appreciate this – it helps to build the relationship;
- Have agreements translated so that there is no misunderstanding. If the other party is responsible for the translation, have it checked to ensure there are no discrepancies which would cause problems later.

Culture is much less obvious. For instance, in general, Spanish and Latin American negotiators will wish to get to know you as an individual before they will trust you in negotiations. Therefore, social meetings over a drink and a meal, and possibly introducing your respective partners, can be a vital step in preparing for a negotiation. Americans, on the other hand, will be straight in there and there may be little room for social interaction.

Which leads me to a vital point – don't stereotype. What I've just said is true with some people – not all. Think of your colleagues. Are they all the same? Of course not, and that applies to all people, everywhere.

There are some excellent publications available which set out the key cultural features in various countries. Build this into your preparation.

possible resources

Learn a few words in the language of the people you are dealing with: "Welcome", "Thank you for inviting us, we're happy to be here", "Good morning, how are you?" This may not lead to a deep and meaningful relationship on its own, but it shows that you are making an effort, and if you are British it pops one of the misconceptions – that we never make an effort and expect everyone to speak English. That's a win!

117. How do you close the negotiation and go for the sale, recognising that a 'win:win' has been attained?

There are tell tale signs to watch for when a negotiation is getting towards the end:

- Concessions from each party become smaller, and less frequent, as each nears their bottom line or gets further from their ideal position;

- Discussion moves from major, significant issues, to smaller and less important ones (the nice to haves, rather than the essentials);
- Parties may use language such as, "The significant progress we have made";
- Confidence levels may visibly increase, reflecting the fact that each side feels that an acceptable solution is becoming inevitable – watch for good-humoured exchanges, smiling, or other positive signs. Depending on the personality of the negotiator, positive signs may manifest themselves more as a reduction in negative signs – less aggression, less head-shaking and the like.

"The real moment of success is not the moment apparent to the crowd."
George Bernard Shaw

Closing a negotiation involves summarising where the talks have got to, and using a phrase such as, "Let's rap this up". Or "Do we have the basis of an agreement?" When to do it is a judgement call but the good news is that it doesn't matter if you get the timing wrong. If there are significant issues which remain unresolved then the other side will tell you quickly enough.

However watch for tactical positions: towards the end of a negotiation is a great time to go in for those little things which, when added together, can make quite a difference but can be quite expensive to concede. Some people refer to this as 'the nibble' – going for something right at the end of the negotiation which the other team may concede simply because they want to close the negotiation. You are less likely to quibble over a minor issue if you are tired, ready to focus on the next challenge, or under time pressure, self-inflicted or otherwise.

Watch out for the 'nibble'.

Imagine that you are selling industrial equipment. You have

pretty much tied up the deal, and the other side says to you, "I think we're about there on cost and delivery time-scales. All that stands in the way is the training. I take it you'll follow the norm and provide ten days training in with the package we've discussed."

This will be delivered as a statement almost, rather than a question – carrying the implication that the answer is yes. However, is this the norm for your industry? Is this how you normally do business? If yes, then fine. If no, then frame the response in an apparently helpful and upbeat fashion:

"We'd be delighted to put in some training. Our normal terms are £x a day but given the size of this deal we're prepared to give you the first ten days at a 20% discount." It's then your choice on whether you negotiate the number of days, the discount level, or both – or whether you make this your only offer. By taking this approach, you are reflecting the overall value of the deal without giving anything away – especially if you've put the price of the training up so that the 'discount' brings it back down to your normal level.

Having finalised the deal, move to the third stage of negotiation which is Thinking Following the Negotiation:

- Document the deal clearly and unambiguously;
- Tidy up any legalities;
- Ensure that all those people who now need to work together to deliver the deal do so;
- Discuss with your team what went well, and what you'd like to do more of; and what went less well and should therefore be avoided next time;
- Celebrate your success, and
- Move on to the next challenge.

118. It seems to me that, in negotiating costs, prices or salaries there comes a point where it seems in danger of becoming bargaining over trivia or even 'nit picking'; so how do you define the difference between important issues, and trivial ones?

We've looked in the previous answer at 'the nibble'. So when is this a tactic, and when is it actually a significant issue?

One of the most liberating concepts you can use in negotiations is to say, "No" – sometimes that boldly, sometimes in a more tactful way. ("I'd like to help you on this, but it isn't something that we can just throw in. We'd need to apply a charge of £x just to cover our costs" – remembering that they won't know what your costs are.) So, if something comes up at any point of the negotiation that doesn't seem to be a significant issue, then try the "No" approach.

If the other team persists with the issue, then either this is tactical, or the matter under discussion is more significant than it appears.

If tactical, why? Ask yourself what possible reason could they have for pursuing this matter? Is it to keep the conversation away from something you want? Are they seeking to slow down the negotiation, and if so why?

If it is not tactical, then seek to establish why this is so important to them. Ask them. If they say that the issue is important to them, and give some sensible reason, then use this to your advantage; by having put a higher value on it, they may be more prepared to trade some concession that is important to you in exchange. Never make assumptions about the perceived value of something to the other party – what might seem minor to you may be substantial to them for reasons you don't know.

Explore possible assumptions and self-imposed limitations.

212

119. What are the pros ands cons of using phone, fax, and e-mail communication, in and around a significant negotiation?

Technology makes life so much easier in so many ways, not least for the negotiator. We'll look at video conferencing in a moment. However, when using the phone, either in a one-to-one conversation, or with multiple parties in an audio conference, there are various things to bear in mind:

- You are denied the ability to read each others' body language. Therefore, take time to ensure that you understand what is being said, and that your words are understood;
- People can be different over the telephone – perhaps more aggressive, because they don't have to cope with the presence of people in the room. Therefore, make allowances for differences in style;
- If speaking on the phone, be aware that phones can and do momentarily cut out – particularly mobiles. There's a huge difference between, "I would be able to agree that," and, "I would not be able to agree that," but if the phone cut out at the wrong moment then there's a gulf between what you said and what was received. Maintain awareness of that possibility at all times, so summarise often to ensure mutual understanding;
- Pauses over the phone feel like an age, whereas in the face to face situation, it is easier to see if someone is thinking – checking their papers, consulting a colleague, or simply reflecting. Give people time to think – don't feel that silences have to be filled by you;
- Be careful to bring in the quieter people on the call, in the same way that you would in a meeting;
- Never trust the 'mute' button. If you need an adjournment, end the call and reconnect later.

possible obstacles

213

Fax and, more usually, e-mail, are great assets. If you are meeting at a distance, then an e-mailed presentation can get you all on the same page quite easily – but you don't have control over the speed with which the other party will go through your slides, so assume they've read the lot before you get on a call with them. The technique of revealing a surprising piece of information at an appropriate point won't work in these circumstances if you've already included it in your presentation.

With e-mail, again there are a few important rules:

• Be exceptionally careful to convey the right sense and meaning in the words you use. When you are thinking, you sub-vocally emphasise certain words or phrases to yourself. However the reader may make a different set of emphases which could change the meaning of what you are saying.

To illustrate this, imagine the following conversation, where the words in italics are emphasised in the way the words are delivered:

"I would *never* willingly agree to that."

Now compare the meaning of that pretty clear phrase with the following:

"I would never *willingly* agree to that." The latter opens up the possibility that you might agree, you just don't want to – and therefore in the negotiation something has to be conceded that will make you become more willing. However the former phrase closes the door on any possibility of agreement. If the words are typed, with no emphasis, then you may not be getting the point across in the way you intend.

- Equally importantly, be very aware of typing mistakes – and this is never more so than with automatic spell correction which helpfully puts in the word the computer thinks you meant – sometimes with disastrous consequences. Consider a one-letter difference between the following two sentences:

"I am not willing to agree to this," and, "I am now willing to agree to this."

- The best way to ensure your e-mails are understood is to follow up with a conversation;
- Finally, remember that e-mails are easily forwarded, and that you have no control over who is going to see them once you've sent them. Therefore, just as some e-mail systems are not confidential between sender and recipient, and you should therefore be extremely wary of e-mailing confidential information, so too the use to which that e-mail is put is outside your direct control. Therefore, be tactful and diplomatic wherever possible, and remember that your reputation and that of your organisation is on show in every e-mail you send.

All of that said, e-mail is a great way to communicate quickly and clearly once the possible pitfalls are understood and avoided.

120. In what way are negotiations by video conference different from face to face?

Video conferencing enables meetings to be pulled together quickly and efficiently, saving time and money on travelling, or seizing opportunities for negotiation that might not otherwise be there because of logistical or time constraints.

Again, there are various points to bear in mind:

- A video conference gives the impression of being like a face to face meeting, but in reality much of the body language is lost, as is some verbal intonation;
- At distance, appreciate that there is a pause as the signal is sent and received – don't misinterpret this either as hesitation, or as a silence that needs to be filled;
- Again, take time to involve those who are quiet – not everyone is comfortable with video conferencing;
- The logistics of the meeting require careful attention. Book sufficient time; there is little more awkward than getting to a pivotal point in a negotiation to find that your time slot comes to an end abruptly;
- Ensure that the lead negotiator on each team is nearest to the camera.

It is always worthwhile having the first meeting face to face, even if subsequent meetings are to be by video. This gives you a good opportunity to build or maintain the personal relationships – side conversations, and social chat, are not easily accomplished by video, so it becomes easier if everyone has met face to face at least once.

Thinking following the negotiation

The work is finished, you've agreed the deal, and days, weeks or even months of frantic effort and energy are over. All you really want to do is go and celebrate your success, and then go home, maybe take a well earned rest, or maybe just get straight into concentrating on your next negotiating challenge.

The temptation to do just that can be immense. However, all great negotiators recognise that the negotiation does not end when you and the other party leave the room.

Firstly, the deal needs to be properly documented and finalised so that what you believe you've all committed to can be effectively set out, and delivered. The more complex the deal, the more important this is – remember that many different people, including people who were never party to the actual negotiation, and over many years to come, may need to understand every aspect of the agreement reached. Equally, the documentation is the last opportunity to ensure that both sets of negotiators have understood perfectly what it is that they think they have agreed.

Secondly, there are massive benefits to be gained from reviewing how successful you have been and through considering what went well and what you would choose to do differently next time. This debrief needs to be neither long nor hard; however it is the single best way to put all the effort you have just spent into one focused direction – to make you an even better negotiator. True, it comes at the time when many people feel least like doing it, but it is an invaluable part of the process of negotiating.

**"In the pursuit of learning every day
something is acquired."
Lao Tzu**

---

121. What do you have to do once the negotiation is over?

The end of the negotiations isn't the end of the work. There are three stages of negotiation, and the final stage – Thinking following the negotiation – is every bit as important as the rest. The urge to walk away after the negotiating is done, leaving the finalisation of implementation arrangements to others, can be strong. But your integrity as a negotiator is judged by your ability to deliver against your commitments, and so this final stage is vital if you are to preserve and enhance your reputation as someone who can deliver.

There are certain tasks that need to happen during this final stage:

• Ensure the agreement you have reached is documented. This may be an exchange of letters, or a formal agreement, or a legally binding contract;
• Ensure that all parties to the agreement are happy with the way it has been documented, that the responsibilities of each party are clearly and unambiguously set out, and that all parties have the same interpretation of the agreement. Remember that some agreements are very long-standing, and what is written now may be relied upon in years to come by people who were not actually party to the agreement at the time;
• Ensure that all the people on your side who need to do things to implement what has been agreed are clear as to their responsibilities and understand what has to be done, and by when;
• Ensure that those who are responsible for overseeing the agreement in operation and that all aspects of the agreement are met, such as appropriate payments being made at appropriate times, have details of what they need.

There is a further key activity, which is often overlooked by less experienced negotiators, and that is to pull the team together to debrief how the negotiation went:

• What was particularly good, and will assist if it is repeated in the future;
• What worked less well and should therefore be avoided in future.

"Being extremely honest with oneself is a good exercise."
Sigmund Freud

Finally, the most important part of all: celebrate your success, thank all of those people who contributed to it, and move on to the next challenge!

122. Can things go wrong even at this late stage?

Not if you've maintained positive engagement right to the final stages.

However things can go wrong at this point. The commonest 11th hour problems are:

- Getting into the detail of documenting the agreement to find that one party has a different interpretation of key aspects of the deal than the other. There are two ways to overcome this: either stick firmly to your interpretation and hope that the other party backs down; or reopen discussions. You can, of course, decide to accept their version of events, but that would depend on how strongly you feel about the issue which is disputed, and whether by changing your position you are detrimentally affecting the deal or the achievement of your goals. Genuine mistakes do get made, but last minute attempts to make changes to a deal can also be tactical in nature, and a last ditch attempt to 'nibble';
- People you are relying on to do things don't deliver. This requires careful hands on management. If you have genuinely over-committed your organisation to something that can't now be delivered, then the sooner you flag this to the other side the better;

219

- The other team don't deliver in some respects. Consider whether this is significant to the deal. If it isn't a deal-breaker, then always convey your displeasure forcefully and in a way that will encourage people to deliver next time. If you do nothing, you may be seen as a soft touch and people may seek to take advantage of your good nature next time. If it is a deal-breaker, then you need to reopen discussions and ensure that this is understood. Depending on the nature of your agreement, you may be able to rely on compensation clauses for non-delivery, or legal remedies. Always bear in mind the impact of legal action on your long-term relationship – sometimes it might not be worth it, even if they are in the wrong technically.

123. What do you do if the other party does not agree with the fine detail in the documentation, even though they agreed in the negotiation?

Happily, this is rare. It is also largely avoidable by following all of the stages of negotiation set out in this book, from preparation, through the negotiations themselves, and into the work you do to close the deal and document it properly.

Occasionally, however, there can be a situation where one party contests some point of detail right at the end. This might be an attempt to 'nibble'. Stick to your position and see if they change their mind.

Otherwise, reopen the negotiation and, in the light of events, decide whether it is in your interests to lose the deal, or even the relationship. However, ensure this decision is a commercial one, and not one driven by emotion – even though it is most vexing to be let down after so much time, effort and money has been invested in a negotiation.

220

If you do make some concessions at the final stage, ensure that you position yourself to take advantage of that in the next negotiation you have with these people – things should never be all one way, particularly when you are doing all the giving and they are doing all the taking!

**"The greatest secret of success in life is for a person
to be ready when their opportunity comes."**
Benjamin Disraeli

CASE-STUDY SCENARIOS AND FURTHER INFORMATION

124. Time to consider: Three scenarios

Opening the negotiation – getting off to a good start

You've done your planning, your negotiating mandate is agreed by those who need to give their authority, you and your team know your roles perfectly, and you have the answers to every issue that you think could possibly come up.

You walk into the room, exchange pleasantries, everyone introduces themselves. You pour yourself a glass of water.

Then what?

Kicking off a negotiation can sometimes be like taking that first shot off a golf tee – everyone is watching, and yet you haven't actually hit a single golf ball today. What if it all goes horribly wrong? What if you mess it up right at the beginning – you set the wrong mood for the meeting, you lose confidence, everyone wonders if you're up to it. In spite of all that preparation – all that time spent thinking about how you are going to make the right start in the negotiations, those hindering thoughts might still be there somewhere at the back of your mind...

The best way to avoid all this is to imagine the helpful scenarios in your head before you get into the room. When you get there, in effect you've done it all before. In truth, reality never quite goes according to a script, but you'll have strengthened your self-belief, and grown your confidence to the point that it can't go wrong for you. You'll even have planned for all those unexpected things that might come up right at the beginning.

223

In planning the opening of a negotiation, there are a few essential questions to ask yourself.

- Who called the meeting? If it was the other side, consider whether it is to your advantage to let them open the meeting;
- Are you buying or selling? This can make a profound difference to how you will want to play the early stages of the negotiation;
- What mood do you want to create? There are circumstances where you might want to be quite robust in your style and language right up front.

Let's look at a few scenarios:

Scenario I

You are attending the meeting in order to buy components for a product which your firm manufactures. You are in a hurry – your normal supplier has let you down and if you do not source these components quickly, production in your plant will have to halt. This will be costly, and will leave you with incomplete and therefore unsaleable stock. This, in turn, will lead you to let down some of your own long-standing and profitable customers. You know that you are working in a strongly competitive environment, and your customers won't stay around too long waiting for your company to get its act together. If your customers go elsewhere, they may well not come back to you. Therefore, you are under enormous pressure to deliver – but not at any cost. Your business cannot afford to buy the components at a premium price because your operation will then be unprofitable, and your already strained cash flow will become unsustainable.

Whilst the language you use will always be your own, matching your style and personality, you might use an opening along the following lines:

"Thanks for fitting us in so quickly – diaries are a nightmare at the moment and if we couldn't have done today this meeting might have been weeks off. That's success for you – all work and no play!"

Or:

"We're here to look at what we might be able to do for each other on the components front – our expansion plans suggest we look at a number of alternative solutions and suppliers. With your reputation, you're right there amongst those at the top of our list."

This first opening subtly addresses the point that you might have moved Heaven and Earth to get the meeting in the diary quickly – but you are acknowledging this whilst giving the implication that your diary is a nightmare – and theirs as well potentially – rather than saying you are in a desperate hurry.

The second possible opening positions the meeting as a review of options on your side. Expansion puts in their minds the potential for a long-term relationship, not just a one-off deal. The potential for repeat orders will, in a competitive environment, put you in a stronger position to get an attractive price.

In a situation like this, plan for the worst possible response. You have opened the negotiation, and the first thing they say is:

"We hear that your usual supplier has let you down. You must be under enormous pressure to replace them or your factory will be grinding to a halt any time soon."

You could try the straight denial – this might be an attempt to test the truth behind an unsubstantiated rumour; or they could well be connected and well prepared. Either way, if they think you are under great pressure to deliver, this puts you at a disadvantage. Consider one of the following responses:

"Who told you that?" delivered in a slightly incredulous tone. Their response will help you judge whether they know the truth or not. Whatever the answer, you could follow up with:

"We decided quite some time ago to carry out a thorough review of our component sourcing operations for a whole raft of reasons. Now is a great time because we're carrying excess stock and things are quite comfortable, so if our existing suppliers decide to take their bat and ball home we've got time on our side."

They may or may not believe you. The point is that you are building a picture to refer to as the negotiation continues:

- You aren't in a particular hurry;
- There is a long-term supply deal up for grabs as you are reviewing your supply arrangements;
- It looks as if you may have anticipated supply problems and so have built up your stock of components, which would be good business practice and will therefore look credible;
- You are looking at a number of options, so it's by no means certain that these suppliers will get any deal at all.

The negotiation should now progress as normal. Even the nightmare scenario – where they know more about you than you wish they did – can be turned to your advantage. Above all, whilst the supplier will wish to push as hard as possible, it is not in their interests to push so hard that your business goes under, because the potential for a long-term profitable relationship disappears.

Scenario 2

Let's use the same situation, but this time you are the supplier. You know that the other side are in a hurry for your components. You are in a position to fulfil this order, and you know that the likelihood of other suppliers being in the same position is remote. Therefore, you are in the strongest position possible. So how do you open the neogitation to get yourself in the best position for your business?

Consider opening the discussion yourself, even though it is not your side who called the meeting. Whether you go first or second, use words along the following lines:

"I've heard about the issues you've had with your component suppliers. We're confident that we can help you through this difficulty and explore ways in which we can all get what we need for the future."

This opening is positioning your company as a key element in overcoming the problems faced by the other side. Whilst you have referred to the supply difficulties you have presented your position as an offer of help, and you have also begun – even at this really early stage – to float the idea that you want to do future business, not just a one-off supplier deal. You are then in a good position to put forward a business solution for the long-term which is good for your company, and good for theirs because it gets rid of the uncertainty over future component supplies.

During the negotiation – getting what you want

Things are progressing well. You have achieved a number of your key requirements, but on some issues you just aren't getting the progress you want. How do you get things moving in the right direction?

Scenario 3

You are purchasing vehicles for your sales force. You have presented your plans regarding your vehicle requirements over the next three years but you want to get more out of the deal, and you are also unclear as to whether you have achieved the best price you can.

Consider throwing something else into the conversation which hasn't so far been on the table:

"This just isn't quite working for me. One of the ideas at the back of my mind is that we could bring our sales fleet provisioning together with our maintenance vehicle supply arrangements – that's as many vehicles again over the course of the contract we're thinking about. I would expect that to have quite an impact on the pricing for the sales fleet. What would that look like?"

You would then be expected to go into some detail about what the maintenance fleet consists of, how long the vehicles are held, and the like. In due course, your question on the sales fleet will be answered, perhaps along the following lines:

"We're actually at our best price for the sales fleet but obviously are very keen to look at the bigger contract."

To which you might respond:

"There would have to be something in it for us. Either the acquisition price comes down or we agree replacement at list less 35% at 60,000 miles."

If something you like the look of is then put forward in respect of the sales vehicles, you might say:

"Let's agree that for the sales cars and we'll guarantee to review our maintenance vehicle sourcing with you by the end of the year." This commits you to nothing other than a conversation some way down the line, but tells you the price at which they could provide the sales vehicles and still turn a profit – it would be most unusual for a supplier to provide any element of such a supply arrangement at less than an acceptable profit margin to them. So if they say;

"We can only do that price if the maintenance vehicles form part of the contract," don't believe it.

Closing the negotiation – ending on a productive note

You have had a wide-ranging conversation, possibly over a number of meetings, and have achieved everything you can reasonably expect to achieve through the negotiations. How do you move beyond the negotiation and wrap things up, whilst ensuring that nothing you've agreed in principle is lost along the way?

Whatever the situation, the following is a great way to bring matters to a satisfactory conclusion for all concerned:

"Let's summarise where we're up to. We've agreed the following..." and then list your interpretation of what's been said. Go on to say:

"That looks like the basis for a deal then. I suggest we document where we're up to, sign it off between ourselves by close of play tomorrow, and move forward from there. Are we agreed?"

Often that's all there is to it. However let us assume that the other party responds as follows:

"We're almost there. But there is a point about delivery. It's only a 30-day turnaround for the first 10,000 units. Anything over that is 45 days."

Depending on whether this is important to you, consider the following:

"We need 30 days on the lot. If that's not achievable it impacts our cost base so we'll have to revisit the figures."

Here, you are subtly implying that the whole deal might have to be renegotiated. This will soon show you whether the attempt to delay delivery for orders above 10,000 units is a negotiating tactic or not. Towards the very end of negotiations each side will often attempt to gain a few concessions from the other, banking on the prospect that the other side is lacking in the motivation to argue back – particularly at the end of a long and tiring set of negotiations.

So do something back. At the end of summarising the points you have agreed in principle, say:

"The only thing between us that I can see is this point about delivery. If we can guarantee a delivery of 20 days on everything, I think we're there."

It's always worth a go.

125. More negotiating skills resources (by Jonathan and Andy)

'How to win in negotiations' is a practical, pocket size guide to 130 hints and tips on getting the most out of your negotiations.

'Negotiating for Results' is a one-hour audio CD in the 'Your Questions Answered' series of interviews with subject experts. This features Jonathan answering many of the questions featured in part five of this book.

'There's Always a Deal' is a 6 CD audio programme which explores the ways in which the Go MAD Thinking System can help anyone, regardless of their level of experience, strengthen their influencing and negotiating skills. The programme gives details and insight into how to develop your ability by sharing the expertise of the authors and of a wide variety of successful negotiators from various backgrounds.

Go MAD About Negotiating training programmes based upon the content of this book, and including the above resources, can also be tailored to the needs of your organisation. For further information please visit the website www.gomadthinking.com or e-mail info@gomadthinking.com or telephone +44 (0)1509 891313.

126. Applying the Go MAD Thinking System at four levels

From reading this book it is easy to think that Go MAD is all about negotiating, but remember Go MAD was not originally developed as a negotiating model even though this has become a powerful application (refer to chapter 8 about the original research). Its broadest application is as a thinking system which provides both structure and flexibility in the following areas:

231

The following chapter provides a brief insight into the broadest application of helping organisations develop a solution focused thinking culture.

127. Leadership thinking and cultural transformation

Imagine if everyone who worked in an organisation shared the same thinking system, with an easy to understand language, aligned to clearly defined business goals. It makes sense! If everyone is equipped to use the same IT system, why not equip people to use the same thinking system?

In addition to Andy's research and writing activities, much of his time is spent working with leaders in organisations developing business improvement and leadership thinking programmes to enable business results to be achieved quicker and more cost effectively. As you might expect, achieving large-scale change can often be quite complex.

> **"The old guard in any society resents new methods, for old guards wear the decorations and medals won by waging battle in the old accepted manner."**
> **Martin Luther King, Jnr**

From 2000 onwards, the team of Go MAD Thinking Engineers have developed and tested ways of embedding Go MAD as a thinking system using a rigorous installation methodology to guarantee measurable results. The Go MAD Thinking System, which you have become familiar with in this book, has been developed into the Go MAD Organisational Development Framework to analyse and facilitate change at a macro level.

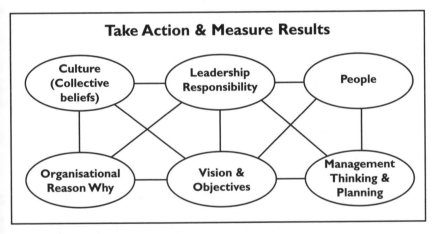

Go MAD® Organisational Development Framework

So, instead of Personal Responsibility this becomes Leadership Responsibility; the People involved include employees, customers and other stakeholders; the goal becomes the Vision; the individual Self-Belief becomes the Culture of the organisation; the Reason Why becomes an Organisational Reason Why (e.g. shareholder value); and Planning Priorities becomes a Management Thinking

233

activity in line with the business objectives and direction given by the leadership team.

Adopting a systems thinking approach to organisational change means that we need to consider the individual elements and their impact upon each other. Potentially there will be a need to take action and measure the results of each element. A different set of questions can now be asked to analyse the macro differences leaders are seeking to make and identify weaknesses in the system.

- What is the organisational reason for seeking change?
- What is the leadership vision?
- How strong is the existing culture to support the vision?
- How is the vision being communicated to managers responsible for the planning and implementation?
- How effectively are the objectives being communicated to other people (employees, customers, suppliers, etc.) to obtain their commitment?

Now we realise that this might all seem a bit much if you only want to apply Go MAD Thinking at a personal effectiveness level. However, there might be a time when your reason why is sufficiently strong to help others, and possibly an organisation, make a greater difference. If that time is now, we recommend you read, 'How to Make A Difference by Transforming Managers into Leaders', by Andy Gilbert & Sally Fagan and, 'How to Save Time and Money by Managing Organisational Change Effectively', by Andy Gilbert.

"Your legacy should be that you made it better than it was when you got it."
Lee Iacocca

If you are a business leader seeking to make a difference and require further information, contact the Go MAD team and we will send you a free DVD of case-study information (email: info@gomadthinking.com).

128. Go MAD information and resources

If you liked the practical style of this book, and are interested in reading further publications written by Andy and the Go MAD team, you might want to consider the following:

How to Make A Difference by Transforming Managers into Leaders
(255 practical tips and ideas to develop your leadership ability.)

How to Save Time and Money by Managing Organisational Change Effectively
(A practical guide to help managers handle people's reaction to organisational change.)

How to Save Time and Money by Managing Meetings Effectively
(101 ways to make a difference before, during and after meetings.)

Go MAD – The Art of Making A Difference
(A powerful guide for achieving personal and business success and a great introduction to Solution Focused Thinking.)

Go MAD About Coaching
(Over 300 powerful coaching questions, plus tips, tools, techniques and templates. The managers' guide for helping others to make a difference.)

Who's Driving Your Bus?

(An easy to read, inspirational story about the power of the Go MAD Thinking System.)

Go To Work On Your Career

(256 pages of tips, tools and techniques to help manage and develop your career.)

Contagious Customer Care

(Easy to read case-studies and practical tips about making a difference.)

59 Minutes to a Calmer Life

(Helpful insights to help reduce stress in your professional and personal life.)

Small Business Big Difference

(Over 200 tested and proven ideas for growing and managing a small to medium-sized business.)

Brain Magic (Book and 6 CD Audio Set)

(Just how does your brain work? 150 of the most commonly asked questions are answered giving you practical tips to living a longer, happier and healthier life.)

To order, or register for our free e-zine, simply visit our website at www.gomadthinking.com or telephone +44 (0)1509 891313.

If you are seeking to make a difference within an organisation and would like to have a discussion about any aspect of applying Go MAD as a catalyst for cultural change, leadership thinking, business improvement or management development then please contact one of the Go MAD Thinking Engineers.

Go MAD Research & Consulting Group
Pocket Gate Farm
Off Breakback Road
Woodhouse Eaves
Leicestershire
LE12 8RS
England
email: info@gomadthinking.com
telephone: +44(0) 1509 891313

NOTES

NOTES

NOTES